TOTAL RESTORATION
Real Stories of Survival and Perseverance from Cottage Grove, Oregon

Table of Contents

DEDICATION

This book is dedicated to all those who have ever felt like giving up. Those who have experienced circumstances in life that have left them feeling hopeless and defeated. Those who feel tormented by past mistakes and failures. Those who are suffering from life-destroying addictions and habits. If you need hope and are in desperate need of a *Total Restoration*, this book is for you!

ACKNOWLEDGEMENTS

I would like to thank Rulon Combs for his vision for this book and for his hard work in making it a reality. And to the people of Living Faith, thank you for your boldness and vulnerability in sharing your personal stories.

This book would not have been published without the amazing efforts of our project manager and editor, Debbie Allen. Her untiring resolve pushed this project forward and turned it into a stunning victory. Thank you for your great fortitude and diligence. Deep thanks to our incredible Editor in Chief, Michelle Cuthrell, and Executive Editor, Jen Genovesi, for all the amazing work they do. I would also like to thank our invaluable proofreader, Melody Davis, for the focus and energy she has put into perfecting our words.

Lastly, I want to extend our gratitude to the creative and very talented Jenny Randle, who designed the beautiful cover for *Total Restoration: Real Stories of Survival and Perseverance from Cottage Grove, Oregon.*

Daren Lindley
President and CEO
Good Catch Publishing

TOTAL RESTORATION

I would like to thank photographer Tom Strongman for letting us use the photo of the rusted 1942 Chevrolet Fleetline on the front cover. It was the perfect photograph for the project. I would also like to thank Carlos and the San Fernando Oldies Car Club for letting us use the photo of the perfectly restored '42 on the back cover; I think it is the most beautiful '42 Chevy in the country today.

Rulon Combs

The book you are about to read
is a compilation of authentic life stories.
The facts are true, and the events are real.
These storytellers have dealt with crisis, tragedy, abuse
and neglect and have shared their most private moments,
mess-ups and hang-ups in order for others to learn and
grow from them. In order to protect the identities of those
involved in their pasts, the names and details of some
storytellers have been withheld or changed.

INTRODUCTION

What do you do when life is careening out of control? When addiction has overtaken you or abuse chained you with fear? Is depression escapable? Will relationships ever be healthy again? Are we destined to be destroyed by neglect or by our environment like the old car on the front cover? Is there any chance that hope or happiness could be restored?

Total Restoration is a process. Whether we are talking about cars, houses or people, restoration takes time. In some cases, quite a lot of time. But I believe that each one of us can experience this process of restoration in our own lives. It *is* possible to become a new person. The seven stories you are about to read prove positively that people right here in our town are becoming new people from the inside out. Whether they've been beaten by abuse, broken promises, shattered dreams or suffocating addictions, the resounding answer is, "Yes! You can become a new person." The potential to break free from these destructive cycles and to enjoy a bright future is within your grasp.

Expect inspiration, hope and transformation! As you walk with these real people from our very own city through the pages of this book, you will not only find riveting accounts of their hardships, you will learn the secrets that brought about their breakthroughs. These people are no longer living in the shadows of yesterday.

TOTAL RESTORATION

They are thriving with a sense of mission and purpose TODAY. All of them are in the process of *Total Restoration*. May these stories inspire you to begin this process in your own life.

FIFTY ROUNDS TO FREEDOM
The Story of Grant
Written by Richard Drebert

My 90-year-old grandmother shifted gears in her daddy's dairy truck. She was 13 again, a Cajun beauty with raven-black hair; early mornings she helped her father milk the cows.

She looked at me with a near-toothless smile, but greeted her little brother. "You gotta pick up hay today, Alvin!"

I nodded. "Okay ..."

Dementia.

I set my glass of Jack Daniels on the nightstand beside her bed and stuffed the .45 automatic into my belt before adjusting her pillows.

I was a newborn baby when this frail woman took me in.

Across the room, Tom Brokaw's voice blared on the evening news, and I turned it to a whisper. Now I could detect the sounds of boots and battering rams or the telephone if police negotiators called again.

I was 42 years old, 250 pounds, 6-foot-2, with fists the size of baseball mitts — and my grandmother's full-time caregiver.

I had beaten and cuffed felons for a dozen years, but

for the last few months I combed Grandmother's sparse gray hair, changed her bedding and fixed her meals.

It was the least I could do for the woman who raised me after her daughter gave me up. I still thought of Grandmother as "Mom."

I closed her door, wishing I was as unaware of *my* reality as she was of hers. Mom's bedroom was positioned in the center of my house, the safest room in a firefight with the SWAT team — that waited for my next move.

My cell phone rang.

"It doesn't have to be this way, Grant. Leave the gun inside and come out …"

"Hey, Mac, why are you even talking to me?" My words felt thick and unwieldy. "I uz a cop, 'member?"

I sucked hard on my joint and held the fumes in for a few seconds. "I'll be out about midnight. I don't wanna kill any of you guys, so stay under cover when I start shootin'."

"Don't do that, Grant. It won't end well …"

"How about you send my wife round with our car to pick up the old lady first? I don't want her in the middle of a firefight."

Mac paused a few seconds. "Negative. We can't risk it."

The Siskiyou County Sherriff's Department reckoned that I would take Doris out — she had reported me to a deputy in the first place.

I hung up the phone and sat down at a computer, bleary-eyed. I typed a spiteful letter to my wife. I printed out a list of Mom's needs and how I thought she should be cared for after I was dead.

A sniper's red dot touched my shoulder. Another laser flicked across the screen, and I decided to move to another room.

బ్బబ్బబ్బ

I was the "abortion that got away," my family used to say. My birth mother was barely 18 and Dad was 16 when they married. The justice of the peace pronounced them man and wife so that no one could call me a bastard when I was born a couple months later.

Mother got a job with the telephone company and gave me to my grandmother. Grandmother had lost her own late-in-life baby, Sammy, to SIDs weeks before I was born, so I came along at just the right time. We needed each other.

Back in Louisiana, Pop (my grandfather) was raised a poor dark-skinned swamp dweller, and Mom (my grandmother) belonged to a well-off family that owned a dairy farm. They eloped and left the bayous when Mom was a teenager. Mom and Pop moved to Oakland, California — a melting pot where people were more open-minded to mixed-race marriages.

Their firstborn son, George, lived at home most of the time when I was growing up. My uncle George was 20 years older than me, but he treated me like his little brother after Sammy died.

TOTAL RESTORATION

My real mother visited Mom, Pop and me after work and on her days off — more often than not unhappy, soused and belligerent. In one memorable episode during an argument, Mother grabbed my little Cajun mom by the throat and dragged her to the floor beside the couch. Screeching and scrabbling sounds bounced off the walls until Pop came and broke up the mother-daughter bout.

Wherever these two women lived and worked, tension electrified their conversations. Mom enforced her demands with sheer will and razor-sharp words. Mother "lost it" without warning, especially after a few beers. Shoving usually preceded her all-out physical assault.

അആആ

At a rangy 6 feet tall, Mother wore her miniskirt like a dare. After years of wreaking havoc upon men, she finally married a high-rise window-washer, my stepdad, who quickly learned to kowtow — or wince at his bruises as he squeegeed the next day.

"Son of a …!"

At the Sears auto service center, Mother pulled up to her favorite gas pump, and so did another woman in a Caddy at the same time. They faced off, bumper to bumper. Neither could reach the gasoline nozzle, and a horn-honking battle escalated to screaming epithets out their car windows.

A wide-eyed boy in the Caddy sat beside his furious

mother, just like me. He looked to be about 12 years old, too.

Suddenly Mother flung open her door. Her high heels click-slapped to the Caddy's open window, and Mother's fist hammered the woman full on the side of her face. Without missing a beat, she grabbed the poor woman's hair and rammed her head into the steering wheel, over and over, honking the horn with every thump.

"The nerve!" Mother seethed as she slid into the seat beside me again. We raced off to another gas station.

The other kid was crying, but it wasn't a big deal to me. I was learning that physical aggression could settle any argument. Mother instructed my conscience to feel no guilt when I, too, beat someone down.

❧❧❧

Mom cooked and cleaned at our parish rectory, Saint Louis Bertrand Catholic Church of Oakland. And she commanded implicit respect from family, priest and parishioner, like a petite fine-edged butcher knife.

I attended Catholic school at Bertrand until middle school, and my best friends all wore priests' collars. Our head parson, Father Ralph, was a jolly self-proclaimed draft dodger, who usually started drinking somewhere around noon. One day *he* had to confess — to Mom.

My toes could barely reach the gas pedal when he agreed to teach me to drive without her permission. On my first memorable lesson, I shifted into reverse as he

TOTAL RESTORATION

"safely" walked behind his precious '66 Mustang to open the passenger-side door. I might have rolled him over, had it not been for a pole on the basketball court.

Mom *did* give her permission to Father Ralph's younger second-in-command, Father Edgar, to take me to peace marches and war protests. When I was about 10, we joined the infamous 19-month Occupation of Alcatraz. We boated to the island to show solidarity with the activists, like the rock band Creedence Clearwater Revival and actors Jane Fonda and Marlon Brando, who protested federal policies dealing with Native Americans.

One day I asked Mom a pivotal question that set the trajectory of my future. It seemed logical that God should be part of my life, outside our Catholic compound.

"Mom, how come we don't have any Bibles in our house?"

The little woman set me straight. "Grant, the priests study the Bible *for* us. It's not your job."

Thereafter, I left religion and God to the priests.

My days of bellying up to the long butcher-block table in Mom's rectory kitchen for snacks ended — but not my confusing childhood.

The only kids in my parish were gang members or wannabes from the Oakland ghetto, and they swaggered in and out of Bertrand's iron gate during the weekdays. I never officially joined any gangs, but it was fun to tag along on their escapades.

"Take it out! Do it!"

The sound of a brick shattering a storefront window felt exhilarating, and hearing the *whiiiiish* as I stabbed the sidewall of a BMW tire took the edge off my own inner rage.

I ran with all kinds of mixed-race kids, but my birth certificate said I was Caucasian.

"How come you act like a white kid?" friends in my mostly black neighborhood asked me. I didn't know, and I didn't fit in.

Who am I?

I resented not having a mother and father I could call my own — and I blamed my hot-tempered mother for chasing my real dad away. One day my family enrolled me in a school away from our ghetto neighborhood to save me from the gang influence. I transferred to Edendale Middle School in San Lorenzo where Mother lived with my stepdad.

During the '60s and '70s, sex, drugs and rock and roll helped me find the identity I longed for. I learned to play the steel guitar — emulating twisted rock gods like Jimi Hendrix and Led Zeppelin's Jimmy Page. My idols could overdose on drugs, spend time in jail or act outrageous in public and people loved them! They possessed personas that fans adored and never suffered consequences. I wanted to be *them*.

I despised my teachers, and in high school I wouldn't have attended classes at all, if it wasn't that I played football. Perpetually stoned and surly, I made my school administrators as miserable as I could.

When I turned 18, my 1970 Malibu burned rubber in the school parking lot for the last time. I felt pretty cool until reality slapped me in the face at home. Pop laid down the law.

"Grant, you have two days to get a job — if you want to live here."

Pop worked for Crocker Bank as a vault supervisor and never missed a day. I headed for the employment office and landed a job in a warehouse.

"So you want to get away from all this?"

In our tattered booth at Nation's Giant Hamburgers, Sergeant Cook, my portly Army recruiter, waved a fleshy arm at Oakland.

I was at my wit's end. After just a year as a dropout, no one wanted me around, including my family. I needed a *change.* Fortunately only misdemeanors showed up on my record, but if I waited much longer …

"Sign me up, Sergeant. What's the easiest job in the Army?"

Sergeant Cook pursed his lips over a drooping cancer stick and smiled. "Military Police, Grant. You'll love it …"

In a matter of weeks I stood in a line of naked recruits, and the doc gave me a grudging pass, though my arches seemed a bit flat. The Army flew me to Alabama for Basic Training, and I adjusted to authority that couldn't be bullied.

No pot here. No booze. And no attitude.

Just follow orders.

I was surprised at how much I loved military structure. I didn't have to figure out what to do each day — it was all laid out for me. But six weeks into boot camp, at 2 a.m., a sergeant rousted me out of my rack.

"Downstairs, Grant."

In a dingy Army office, I saluted sleepily at a chaplain and my commander. The chaplain handed me an envelope with tickets home.

"Your mother is gravely ill. You need to fly to Oakland right away …"

Mother had been at the phone company when she complained of a horrible headache. Suddenly blood gushed from her nose and ears before she collapsed. Diagnosed as a cerebral hemorrhage, my birth mother stayed on life support for weeks after I flew back to boot camp.

I didn't care. The family could deal with deciding when to pull the plug. I had work to do. I was behind in my training and had to catch up.

Most of the men in the military police angled for a job in law enforcement after they received their honorable discharge from the Army. Not me. I decided not to make the Army my career, but I stayed in the Army Reserves in Oakland.

I had served my country for three years before renewing my acquaintance with the Bertrand rectory housekeeper's daughter, Jean.

TOTAL RESTORATION

No one supported our marriage. Not Mom, not Pop — and her parents *hated* the idea. On our way to Reno to elope, I stared at Jean's beautiful, relaxed face as she slept in the seat beside me — thinking.

If I had any decency or really cared for the woman, I'd turn this car around.

Instead I woke my girlfriend in Reno where we said our vows, feeling in my gut that our marriage was a stupid mistake. But I wanted to feel normal. Something inside me yearned to discover love and purpose outside of my selfish, unfulfilled heart.

In less than a year, our families clashed one too many times, and I left Jean. We landed an annulment, and Mom and her priests were happy it didn't say "divorce" on the papers.

ॐॐॐ

Uncle Ray, Pop's brother, was my role model when I was in my mid-20s. He was a career machinist at American National Can, and his life principles fit with my own. He had a family and was well-respected in the community — but no one got in the way of his booze and women on the side. He got me a position as a machinist's helper — which petered out in two years when the economy went bust.

"How long are you goin' to wait for National Can to call you, Grant?"

My carousing friend, Del, an Oakland police officer, sat at the bar with me and handed me a napkin with a name and phone number on it. "Go see Sergeant Rowen. Stop dreaming about being a machinist. You need to be a cop."

"Maybe I will," I said and made up my mind the next day. I called the sergeant and set up an interview. Sergeant Rowen was a straight-talking officer who read me like a book. And I didn't pull any punches, either.

"Look, I've always been a jerk, Sergeant. I grew up here, and when I was young I was on the wrong side of the law most of the time."

Rowen smiled. "Remember, we're talking about *Oakland*, with one of the highest crime rates in the country. The department isn't looking for Boy Scouts. We're looking for men who can handle the streets."

He paused, his dark eyes boring into me. "I think you're one of those guys."

Suddenly I was sold on the idea. I hauled away a stack of glossy brochures and mandatory paperwork, and on my drive home I realized that I might have to change my attitude: *I hated Oakland cops.*

I passed my academy training in Criminal Law, Firearms, Arrest and Control Techniques, Community Relations, Vehicle Operations, Traffic Enforcement and First Aid.

I found that the Department had two kinds of officers: natives, who were raised in the Oakland area and understood the streets; and non-natives, cowboys who wanted to experience the Wild West.

We natives didn't drink with the cowboys after shifts much. Cowboys were using the Oakland Police Department to build resumes for a cushy job in Oregon or Idaho. With our record number of homicides, after about three years an officer could point to his experience in Oakland and become a homicide detective on some small police force.

As for me, I had finally achieved Rock Star Status. My badge gave me license to do whatever I wanted, to whomever I pleased on my turf. The Department gave me cart-blanche to exercise any and all methods of force to control a suspect. Before Taser-like weapons were commonly used, we applied batons, boots and fists to subdue someone. Our training manual instructed us in the proper "escalation" of force — but I often skipped to an old-fashioned beat-down technique if a suspect resisted. In my first two years, none of my commanders censured me for my methods of arrest, because it was considered Department protocol.

After my probationary period, I finally let the morose, angry Grant loose among my fellow officers, most of whom I had little respect for. I snubbed officer's gatherings and scorned Department politics and favor swapping. My disgust for supervisors rivaled the contempt that I reserved for the grossest criminals on the street.

Several officers who lived outside "inner city" Oakland were hooked on various drugs, like cocaine, meth and marijuana. They didn't dare venture into my ghetto streets for fear of other police officers seeing them with dealers. I lived in the ghetto area, and no one even questioned why I was there.

I milked my connections and carried drugs to the suburbs for my officer "friends." The money was good, and I had no qualms about committing felonies while wearing my uniform. And with my police badge, dealers supplied me all the drugs I needed to feed my own addictions.

I sat in my living room with a beer in my hand when the video of Rodney King's beating by Los Angeles police officers hit the evening news. King was an African-American, apprehended by Los Angeles police officers after a high-speed chase. He resisted arrest, and as per Department protocol, the officers escalated force as they saw fit.

"Just stay down! Stop resisting, and *they'll* stop!" I hollered at the TV.

He didn't. The officers, assuming that he was high on PCP, "power stroked" his body with side-handle batons until he finally lay still on the pavement. None of the officers realized that the incident had been videotaped by a man on a nearby balcony. News stations all over the country aired portions of the video, stretching racial tensions to the breaking point.

The police officers were charged with assault with a deadly weapon and use of excessive force. After their trials the next year, all officers were acquitted, triggering riots on the West Coast and in other cities that killed 53 people and injured more than 2,000.

Looting, assaults, arson, murder.

My hometown exploded, too. In April of 1992, I worked long shifts at the Oakland City Jail after we conducted "sweeps" to clear the streets of violent types before the anticipated verdict. The Oakland jail boiled with hatred, and few of us officers obtained necessary backup as we marched suspects into overcrowded cells.

It was the evening of the controversial verdict, now called Rodney King Night, that I escorted a cocky young inmate to a dorm-style holding cell. He was 18 and built like me — without the spare tire growing around his middle. When he cut loose with his first haymaker, no other officers were in the room. He telegraphed his first blow, and I gathered my rage to put him down.

Cheers in the dorm grew louder as inmates watched the Oakland "pig" getting butchered.

It was payback for Rodney.

My drubbing seemed like hours as I hung on to consciousness. With my last burst of strength, I used a Judo move to trip him, and he fell to the concrete. My knees jammed his sides, and I finally stunned him long enough to gain my feet — and my boots pounded his head like a soccer ball until he lay still.

But what was "acceptable" procedure by us Oakland cops *before* Rodney King's beating had become police brutality overnight — even within the Department.

No one had informed me ...

Cameras inside the dorm cell captured the whole grisly fight — and I couldn't talk my way into just a reprimand.

"I did what you guys trained me to do!"

My sergeant talked to me like *I* was the perp.

I laughed sardonically. "Whatever happened to 'watching a brother's back'?"

"Things are different now, Grant. The police union rep will be in touch. Internal Affairs is investigating you for 'excessive use of force.' I need your badge and gun. You're on suspension until further notice. Good luck. I wouldn't want to be in your boots right now."

Without my badge, I felt naked on the streets, and no one knew the depths of my depression. Panic attacks assailed me. I felt my personal code of "no limits, no conscience" weakening, and I self-medicated with drugs and alcohol. After several months, my ordeal ground to a gut-wrenching conclusion.

Brawling "by attorney" and defended by the powerful police officers' union, the Oakland Police Department reinstated me with full benefits. My attorneys successfully threw the blame for the incident upon the OPD and its training practices. But my superiors never forgot that I had sullied the reputation of the vaunted OPD.

క్తిక్తిక్తి

Doris worked as a correctional officer at the OPD and her son, Danny, needed a father. Every cop who knew us warned Doris that I wasn't "normal" marriage material. She was several years younger than me, and we had a standing joke that if I didn't marry her, I could at least adopt her.

Doris and I had two things in common: our addictions to drugs and alcoholic, dysfunctional relatives. We bought a big house together to make a home for Danny, and we seemed almost happy during the year after our wedding.

Officers that I worked with sometimes quipped about "going postal," a phrase coined in the '80s and '90s after several stress-related killing sprees in workplaces. In the second year of my marriage, I began identifying with those killers, who murdered superiors because they felt psychologically shoved over the edge. Every night that I patrolled the streets, I teetered close to a breaking point.

And at home, Doris and I fought, pounding on each other verbally and sometimes physically. It wasn't unusual to see OPD officers standing at our door at 3 a.m. answering a domestic violence call. Neighbors who reported the screams watched from behind their curtains as uniforms smoothed things out between two of their own.

"Hey, Grant, just let us talk to Doris to make sure that Danny and her are okay, and then we'll go ..."

Before I snapped and killed myself or everyone around me, I decided to quit the OPD — and defuse somehow. Doris had resigned some months before me and ran a successful daycare facility in our home. But every evening

Doris' alcoholic, combative relatives *invaded.* To me, they were as omnipresent and unwelcome as bedbugs.

At the brink of divorce, Doris and I decided to take a full day to hash out a plan to patch up our relationship. After hours of arguing, we agreed that we would sell off everything and move to a small town far away — without her relatives in tow. In fact, they would *never* darken our doorway again.

"I can walk away and never see you again, or you can agree to my terms, and we can save our marriage. You're free to meet your family anywhere else but in our home. And Doris: You're making this promise in blood."

Capitalized by profits from selling our house and intoxicated over the prospect of leaving our problems in Oakland, we moved to a little ranching community in Northern California called Hilt.

Her relatives were furious.

৯৯৯

Picturesque. Timber and pastures. Surreal solitude.

"Mom," now frail and needy, had come to live in paradise with the three of us, and due to her dementia, the State paid me to care for her full time. Danny attended school only three miles from our split-level home, at a one-room "*Little House on the Prairie*" schoolhouse.

We had one neighbor, barely in waving distance, and Doris found a good job as a nurse in Yreka, 22 miles away. For the first time in my life, I could smoke my cigarettes on the deck in cool morning tranquility, watching red-winged blackbirds and blue jays patrol the yard for insects. I had stockpiled Jack Daniels — and pot, using a dealer close to the family — and I didn't have to conserve much. At night, Doris and I smoked our marijuana together and had a few drinks — and the next day we did it all over again. Orderly, routine — it was a lot like my life as an Army MP.

My absurd bliss lasted for two months.

One cold morning I fed Mom and got Danny off to school, and Doris and I were enjoying a cup of coffee and cigarettes. Danny's birthday was a couple of days away, and she had planned a party.

We sat in our bedroom talking over our day off together, and suddenly she said, "Grant."

She wore a hint of a smile. "I really don't care about our agreement. My family will be here for Danny's birthday party." She paused to enjoy my reaction. "And there is nothing you can do about it."

My mind jumped from reason to rage as I watched Doris rise like a triumphant kitten and pad softly into the hallway. We had sold all that we acquired in Oakland to invest in our country dream home. My little Cajun Mom lay in her bed with the TV blaring, waiting for "Alvin" to feed her lunch.

I felt trapped. *Betrayed.*

"Someone" inside me suddenly turned paradise to hell. I reached into my nightstand, gripped my .45 pistol and followed Doris down the hall. No need to chamber a round. It was always ready to fire. Doris wheeled around at the end of the hall, spoiling for an expected fight. She had no time to register shock as I jammed the .45's muzzle into her chest. She fell to the floor, and I straddled her. I placed the barrel of the gun to her forehead and cocked the hammer back.

"What do you have to say now?"

I didn't "see" Doris anymore — only a perp who was trying to wreck my life. In 12 years with the OPD, I had never fired my weapon in a shootout, but this time I fully intended to kill the offender. I stood over Doris, and slowly, like Bertrand's church bell, reality softly tolled.

I was a former cop assaulting another former cop with the intent to kill. Alive or dead, Doris would ruin me, and my mind reeled as I left her on the floor, shaking.

Gun Crime, Do Time.

In the kitchen I cursed and grabbed a Budweiser from the fridge and a bottle of Jack Daniels from the cupboard.

No one knows me in Siskiyou County. This time I have no OPD brothers to help me sweep my screw-up under the rug.

I downed a shot of whiskey, then another. I chased them with beer and felt the burn inside my empty belly. I was glad Danny was at school. Doris approached slowly, tears streaming.

"It's going to be okay, Grant," she stammered. She sat down at the end of our big glass dining room table. She eyed the .45 lying on the table top in front of me. "We can work this out, hon."

She sounded like — a cop trying to talk down a bridge jumper. I tossed down another shot and looked her in the eye.

"You're lying. We both know that it's not going to be 'okay'."

My apologies couldn't clear the air this time — and I *wouldn't* go to prison as an ex-cop. And even if I survived incarceration, I could never live the rest of my life as an ex-convict. It was better that I blow my brains out …

I drank until the Jack bottle was empty and started on another at 3 p.m. It was time to get Danny from school.

"I … I gotta go, Grant."

"I know."

Ranchers always wondered why in tarnation a sheriff's deputy needed to patrol the back roads of rural Hilt every three weeks. It seemed a waste of tax dollars. But I thank God that on the day I contemplated suicide, a deputy stopped to assist a frantic woman near Hilt's little schoolhouse.

I had lost control of my future, but God had not.

૰૰૰

Next to the .45 on the glass tabletop, my cell phone rang. "Grant. This is Siskiyou County Deputy Lance. I know you're ex-OPD, and I'm talkin' to you like a brother officer. Look out your window, and you can see me here with your wife. She's real scared for you, Grant."

I stared out the window.

"Why don't you clear your weapon, and leave it on the table. Come out, and let's talk before 500 units get here and gum up the works."

Deputy Lance had parked his car near the entrance of my long drive about 150 yards away, but I knew that a half-dozen patrol cars stood by just out of sight, down the road.

"I'm not going to do that, Depuddy."

"Well, you know I can't just leave. If you change your mind, give me a call on your wife's cell. You know what's going to happen next."

The crisis had escalated to an official "standoff." The officer on the scene judged me to be a danger to myself and the elderly woman inside the house.

I watched an armored vehicle roll up and disgorge SWAT personnel. Other officers were burning up phone lines to OPD to obtain intel on me.

Is Grant the kind of man who will die in a shootout rather than give up?

Siskiyou County Officers spoke to people who had known me since the academy, and Officer TJ, an old graveyard patrol partner of mine, summed up their feelings about me.

"Grant's a great guy, but he once told me over coffee that if he were ever cornered, he would *never* give up his gun. He would go down in a blaze of bullets rather than surrender. Don't try to rush the house! Someone will die."

TOTAL RESTORATION

It was well past midnight, and I was drunk and high, but I knew where every bulletproof vest was located in my yard. Mom seemed to be living in the present at the moment, and I stumbled through a plan to coax her safely to the officers outside.

Mom stopped me dead.

"It's freezing out there! I don't go outside when it's so darn cold. You know that."

"But Doris is out there, Mom. She's gonna take you to dinner."

I stood by the open door, ready to help her down the long flight of stairs into the garage. She looked dubious, then *stubborn*.

"Nope."

If I could carry her down the stairs, I might be able to push the button to lift the garage door and scurry back into the house — *if* I wasn't so drunk.

Too late.

Mom made a beeline for her bedroom. I closed the door.

By 2 a.m., Mom was asleep, and it was time.

Blinding spotlights glared at my windows, and laser sights found every gap in the curtains. The sheriff hadn't cut off power to the house, because of the elderly woman inside, and on the computer I left a rambling letter of explanation.

My cell phone lit up, and I let it ring. I racked a shell into the chamber of my 12-guage and opened the door between the kitchen and garage. At the bottom of the stairs I sat down, nursing half a can of beer. The .45 in my belt pressed my kidney uncomfortably, and I shivered from the Mossberg's cold steel across my lap.

What next?

I sat in the cold dark, while Father Edgar's words handcuffed themselves to my inebriated brain.

"Suicide is the only sin that God will never forgive, Grant."

But is what I am doing really suicide?

After a few rusty Hail Mary's and Our Fathers, I said out loud, "God? I don't know if you're real. I've really screwed up my life, and it looks like I might be committing suicide-by-cop. Not too sure … and if I kill one of these country cops, I hope you forgive me …"

I had no idea how powerful my crude little heartfelt prayer was. I understand now that I tapped into God's *mercy,* available for all of us.

I hit the "up" button to lift the garage door, and slowly, slowly it rose as lasers turned my carport into a discotheque. The mercury vapor light above the driveway outside illuminated my path, and I stopped below it, trying to orient myself for a few seconds. The garage door closed behind me, as slushy rain pelted my face. I squinted at a raspy voice coming from behind a bright spotlight.

"Drop your weapon!"

I ignored Mac completely. "Do it! Shoot! What are you guys waiting for?"

"Grant, it doesn't have to end this way! Put it down."

TOTAL RESTORATION

I choked out, "If you're not going to do it, *then* …" and jammed the barrel of the 12-gauge under my chin.

That's when the sky fell.

Flash grenades exploded all around me, and shotguns unloaded several beanbag rounds. The projectiles hit me, rendering one of my arms useless. Another grenade went off behind my head and shattered the mercury vapor light above me. Everything went black, and the blast shoved me forward. I trained the barrel of my shotgun at the spotlights and fired back, round after round, like a madman.

From three directions rifle and pistol muzzles flashed — live rounds.

A sniper in a tall tree fired the single operative bullet, and it struck my left hip and then pierced my right leg. I fell to the pavement and grabbed at the .45 in my belt, but suddenly I was Rodney King — times 10. Someone kicked my pistol away, as boots, knees and rifle butts descended on me.

Fifty rounds were officially accounted for after our firefight. Slivers and holes stippled the garage door — around my silhouette. Either all the military-trained SWAT marksmen (except one) had missed their target — or God had granted me a second chance at life.

In the weeks following, as I examined pictures with my attorney, I chose to call it dumb luck.

ॐॐॐ

FIFTY ROUNDS TO FREEDOM

At the county jail I refused protective custody, knowing that the moniker "ex-cop" would haunt me after my trial or plea deal, when I served my life sentence in a California penitentiary. As a courtesy to a brother officer (albeit a disturbed one), the Siskiyou County guards and deputies kept my law enforcement past out of the press and jail gossip.

The judge threw me into general population, and for a couple months, I pondered my future like a dog worries a bone: five consecutive 25-to-life sentences, plus 130 years for trying to kill police officers — and other gun-related charges.

The district attorney wouldn't budge on his first and only plea offer: "Forty-five straight years. Take it or leave it. You'll never get anything better from us."

Standing before the judge in my orange jumpsuit, I respectfully declined. "I'm 42 years old, Your Honor. If I take this deal, I'll die in prison. I'd rather go to trial."

A top-notch attorney took my case at a reduced rate, because he was fascinated by my story. The only case law he could find relating to my situation dated back to the 1800s.

Modern stand-offs usually ended with an offender surrendering or shot to death. I had refused to surrender and survived 50 rounds fired by expert marksmen.

ॐॐॐ

TOTAL RESTORATION

I hated the constant noise at the Siskiyou County Jail. Belching, screaming, coarse humor, laughter, rage, singing, babbling ...

I sat in the Siskiyou County Jail, craving relief from the unceasing racket in general population. Suddenly the loudspeaker crackled.

"Line up at the door to attend church services ..."

Church means peace and quiet — and maybe cookies. I'm in.

No one moved to the door but me.

No priest collars, no chants. Just straight talk from a guy who looked like a 70-year-old Marlboro Man. Pastor Ron wore cowboy boots and doffed his Stetson on a chair before he talked about things like Jesus, the Holy Spirit and eternity. It all went right over my head. And no cookies — but I soaked in peace and quiet for about an hour.

"Hey, you boys come back next week."

Ron grinned, and I sensed that he was as genuine as the smokes in my pocket.

I did return, and after his preaching, sometimes a few hard-cases discussed religious stuff. In a few weeks of patrolling this strange, new beat, I traveled from "Not a chance, preacher" to "What's this Jesus thing all about?"

I shot a question at Ron. "I've been coming here about a month now, and I sure don't feel no Holy Spirit. Why is that?"

Ron explained, and nothing sunk in. But then a little wiry inmate with a worn-out Bible smiled and leaned close to my ear. He said, "Hey, bro, when the Holy Spirit comes inside you, you're going to know it. That's all I can tell you."

I responded with "Whatever." But his words gnawed at my soul for days.

Two weeks after my question about the Holy Spirit, I sat in the back of the jail chapel, fidgeting. As Ron talked, I began to feel unhinged, like I could see myself in a mirror for the first time. What I saw sickened me, and I knew I needed saving — or I was lost, now and forever.

Ron was asking us to stand and "make a decision for Christ," but I just sat jiggling my knees, staring at the floor. Suddenly, I felt two strong arms encircling my shoulders — but no one was anywhere near me.

Compassion, peace, joy awareness of God — soaked through my jumpsuit and into my heart. I experienced a father's love for the first time in my life.

Stunned by the beyond-natural experience, I wondered what this old cop-turned-convict needed to do next.

The Marlboro Man came over, and I said, "Thanks, man."

He said, "Praise Jesus, Grant. Praise *Jesus* ..."

I wasn't the only one to shed tears over my exciting change of heart that week. Doris came to visit, and during our conversation, I told her about my experience with God. I had so much to explain to her and so many things to ask forgiveness for.

"I accepted Jesus into my heart, Dor. I'm really born again! You know, a new person inside."

She nearly fell off her chair, laughing. "Born again? Like the hocus-pocus that Jesus Freaks peddle on the streets?"

I was smiling, too, patiently trying to help her see that I wasn't joking. Then it sank in all at once: *I was a changed man.* Tears filled Doris' eyes.

"Whatcha crying for, hon? It's something to celebrate. I really feel free!"

Doris wiped her nose, glancing around her at the concrete walls and bars. She shook her head and stood to go. "Obviously, Grant, you're going crazy in here. And … I feel so sorry for you. Don't you know that Jesus could never accept someone like you?"

Her words cut me — but I understood. Only weeks earlier, I would have said the same thing.

I looked into my wife's eyes as a husband for the last time that day. She stopped visiting me, and she and Danny moved south, away from our corrupted dreams. Mom ended up in a state-run nursing home. And though I faced dying in prison as one of California's prison "elders," my life had really just begun.

The district attorney who offered me "45 years straight time; take it or leave it," retired to Florida. The DA's assistant quit, too, for a better job in another county. Then two other Siskiyou County District Attorneys moved away, leaving a brand-new DA from Los Angeles with loads of cases and temporary assistants.

My attorney had lunch with the new DA to "familiarize" him with my case.

"I don't want to get your hopes up, Grant, but …" (he always started any positive reports this way) "with the new DA we might have a chance at a better plea deal."

Living on the wrong side of prison bars, I had placed my future in God's capable hands — and left it there. I had even stopped carrying my legal pad to take notes at meetings. Jesus had instilled an unnatural peace in my heart about who would be my judge, prosecutor, witnesses and jury. My rescuer was in charge of my upcoming trial — if it happened at all.

But in a miraculous turn of events, God began using a battering ram on the iron gates separating me from freedom. I received three new plea offers in two months.

Twenty-four years, then 18 years.

Then eight years — and I took it!

ॐ ॐ ॐ

These days I encourage and teach young people at Living Faith Assembly of God in the rural community of Cottage Grove, Oregon. In the eyes of some of these young men and women I glimpse a reflection of myself, and I wonder who else is mentoring them through life. A violent mother or father? An immoral uncle? Does an inner rage churn beneath their smiles? What kind of man or woman will they grow up to be?

I used to ask my birth mother why my father never

visited us, and she told me that he wasn't a bad man, but that they just didn't "get along." The explanation only whetted my appetite to know him, and as I grew into my teens, I felt abandoned.

One day I ran across news clippings that Mom kept, describing Dad's shootout with federal agents near Mexico. Dad had been muling (smuggling) heroin across the border. Knowing about my father's life choices influenced my own.

Today I drive across historic bridges in Cottage Grove a free man but an ex-felon. Tears sometimes well up as I travel any highway I choose. My past life of crime and violence doesn't merit the beauty and relationships God has gifted me with.

I am grateful that I ended my sentence at California State Prison, Solano, because God proved himself to me there. With time served, I spent a little more than three years in a facility designed for 2,600 inmates, but housing 4,200.

Riots, thefts, bribery, drugs, gangs, perversions, rape, stabbings, murder ...

I lived *in* this hellish prison system, but I never became part of it. God protected me every hour, and I worked with a ministry team of pastors who had been sentenced to prison themselves for a variety of crimes.

We taught Bible classes to abused men. We loved and prayed for officers and inmates like *I* used to be: men who abused others.

And though I dared not tell *anyone* that I was a former cop, I used my experience on both sides of the law to nudge men toward a Holy Spirit prison transformation like mine.

Behind the prison pallor and sneer, behind the dead-man's stare and badge, every man and woman needs God to save them from themselves.

Sadly, my little Cajun mom passed away while I served time at Solano, and I came out of prison with two heavy strikes against me. I faced a restrictive four-year parole, including unannounced visits from a supervising officer. In my mid-40s, graying, jobless and rejected by society, I had lost everything.

But God is compassionate, loving and *merciful.*

Difficult months passed, and I was blessed with a good job working as a ranch hand. One day my parole officer demanded proof of my sobriety (in a container), and I asked him, "Is there any way we can speed up my release from parole?"

He looked at me, amused. His reply dripped with sarcasm. "Get real, Grant. You're a violent ex-felon. No way *that's* gonna happen."

Three weeks later, my P.O. knocked on my door again.

"Hey, man, you wanna get off parole for good?"

He's jerking your chain, Grant. Easy …

The old Grant would have decked the man, but I calmly said, "That's not funny to a guy like me."

"I may joke around, but not about something like this."

TOTAL RESTORATION

He handed me a manila envelope with papers to sign and recommendations that my parole be stamped "Early Discharge!"

For months, my parole officer had been driving by my church on his way home from the office. He took note each time he passed, that my old pickup was parked at church whenever I wasn't at work.

Within about a year after my prison term ended, I was a completely free man.

I've been married to a beautiful, understanding woman for five years now, and we live in a home where God's peace rules our hearts. I'm a 53-year-old foster dad, and children's voices echo in our house all day long.

Behind razor-wire fences God became *my* loving father, and now, as a free man, he mentors me as a son.

NEVER ALONE
The Story of Victoria
Written by Lori McClure

It was a chilly Oregon day in 1966, and we knew it would be the same as always. We piled our three little bodies into the icky green Chevy Corvair and headed to Fall Creek. Mom let us out and drove on, not wanting to be bothered with three little daughters. We minded her — hoping not to be left again.

"I might come back. I might not." She was very matter-of-fact and cold about the situation.

The door shut behind us, and we watched her drive away, wondering when or if she'd return. As the cool breeze blew, my sisters and I huddled together exactly where we'd been dropped off. We didn't wander for fear we'd miss Mom if she chose to retrieve us. Frightened, we warmed each other and waited as Marcia, my eldest sister at all of 11 years old, comforted and consoled Julie and me, 6 and 3 years old, respectively.

We felt like Hansel and Gretel trapped alone in the forest to find our own way, left to be destroyed by the evil witch. Or was Mother the evil witch? Sometimes I wondered if she was trying to annihilate us all.

This time she did come again for us, and we re-entered our shuttle home only to fall back to the duty of staying hidden and out of the way. Why did we irritate her so?

TOTAL RESTORATION

Why did she treat us like furniture or accessories? It was best to stay away from her, and stay away is what we did.

☙☙☙☙

I watched quietly while my mother and father lifted my new baby brother, Kyle, out of the car, the baby everyone was upset about. Spring hung in the air this March day in 1967, with a sweet pea fragrance following after us all, but only one thought raced through my mind: *One more sibling has arrived to share the burden of living in our sad house.* There were now five of us for my mother to pick on, five children to take the heat: Marcia, David, Julie, me and Kyle. Maybe there would prove to be safety in numbers.

I longed for wholeness, to be nurtured and found in a family of love. But our home held little more than emptiness, despite the number of people living inside. As I grew older, my journal kept my thoughts for me when I needed to be heard. I looked for God in those pages. I poured out my thoughts to him, hoping he heard my prayers.

☙☙☙☙

In the winter of 1969, a glorious blanket of snow fell upon our neighborhood. Our world hid under four feet of white bliss, and for the first and only time, we acted as a family for a few short days. The elements forced us to work together helping Dad fix the patio that had caved in under the weight of our heavy snowfall. School closed, and even chores became playful. We walked to the store to get supplies and food. We worked together like a family should work together. We were a family, my idea of family, the family I always wanted to be.

But our temporary familial fun dissolved with the sun because families like ours go back to old patterns once they can't be forced to work together for the sake of survival. We embraced a different kind of survival in that house with the green shag carpeting always needing to be raked, the one with the big backyard and Japanese garden with white rocks and waterfall Mom somehow never forgot to nurture.

అతిఅతిఅతి

The fighting always increased near the holidays. Dad often ended up home alone, and Grandma came to pick us up. During this particular Christmas, my parents were fighting again when I found myself in the warmth of Grandma Violet's neat, nice and organized living room.

My 10-year-old arms wrapped around the softest, sweetest, most beautiful stuffed panda bear I ever saw. He was all mine, my own little distraction presented to me by my grandmother. Now, I had my own little one to nurture. I could take care of him and love him and be the mommy he needed. That stuffed panda bear gave me my childhood. I could be a little girl lost in play instead of a little girl lost in adult problems. When I tended to my cozy panda bear, my tiny imaginary world was impervious to the cares around me.

❧❧❧

I was in the sixth grade when I entered outdoor school camp. Activities were well underway, and this day, I sat with a roomful of campers in a dark room situated in circles on the floor. He came and found me before I ever realized what was happening. One of the high school counselors was close, so close, too close. His hands slid under the blanket draped over us, and he touched me.

Not only did he visit me in those dark rooms, but he also visited my cabin late at night. If he said it was okay, then it must be okay. And being chosen was better than being ignored. Besides, out of everyone in the camp, he chose me. This was what attention was. This is what you had to do for it. This was normal. The equation was now clear. Sex equaled love.

❧❧❧

As my days stretched on, the emptiness inside me spanned painfully wide. The survival of the lonely goes unnoticed because our battle scars stay hidden, scars of the forgotten, the overlooked, the unseen.

The mini carton of milk waited in front of me on the school cafeteria lunch table. My 14-year-old self sat with two other friends in the midst of lunchroom chaos as I chased 10 to 15 aspirin tablets down with the universal symbol of childhood — chocolate milk. I sat and waited for something bad to happen, but the only thing affected was my hearing. My soul still sat shattered, empty, aching.

Why didn't something bigger happen to me? Why didn't God want to take me when I'd prayed and asked him to let me die? *Why, God?*

Living in a world where mothers refused to mother, where my mother refused to mother me, hurt too deeply. With each new day, the knife of her rejection penetrated further into my heart. I didn't know how many more days I could continue running nowhere in this hamster wheel of solitude.

ॐॐॐ

Mom took turns being mad at us. This time it was Marcia's turn. Mom was so angry with Marcia, she refused to attend her high school graduation. Mom also refused to even let Marcia have her belongings to get ready for the special occasion, so my sisters and I threw items out the window, one by one, for her to catch. Just another normal day around our house.

Thankfully, Grandma came and took us to Marcia's graduation, but the day stood as another reminder Mom was never there for us when we needed her, ever. But Grandma was, and she would take us to church and out to lunch, and she invested time in us we so desperately needed.

TOTAL RESTORATION

᷍᷍᷍

Grandma walked us into a packed and darkened Assemblies of God church in Eugene. People fell down everywhere, and when they did fall, someone came by to lay a towel over their legs. When people weren't falling down, they talked funny. Even Marcia started to talk funny, and I thought she might be possessed.

On the way home in the car, Marcia wavered between talking plainly and speaking in what seemed like gibberish. As strange as the evening was, I believed Grandma when she told us everything was okay. Though I didn't understand exactly what had happened, and it was the first time I'd seen anything like it, I sensed there was something real about it all.

᷍᷍᷍

High school graduation came and went, and I was determined to move on with my life. As a child, the dentist terrified me because he was mean. He'd swear and yell and throw things. I cried and jumped out of the chair and even threw up on the dentist as I was trying to get away so he couldn't work on my teeth.

However, one day, my fears fell away when a new dentist took time to comfort me when he didn't have to. He was so kind, and I suddenly knew what I wanted to be when I grew up. I would be a dental assistant. My dream was still alive, despite my mother's words ringing in my head against me.

"You can't do that. You'll never make it into that program, Victoria."

I proved her wrong when I was accepted the first year I applied to a dental assisting program. Fear crept in with the realization I would be the first in my family to further my education beyond high school, but my father agreed to pay my way. I successfully completed the program, and I was proud to be the first one from my class to get a job. Life was good.

కీకీకీ

"Let's get out of the house!" My roommate, Lori, was desperate for a change of scenery, so we headed out for the night. We soon found ourselves in a local bar so crowded we couldn't find a place to sit. We crashed an already occupied table. That's when I met Gary, and before I knew it, we were spinning together on the dance floor. We connected instantly, stayed out all night and continued on to breakfast together.

Our relationship escalated quickly until Gary started having doubts. He couldn't decide if he wanted to marry or not. But I knew this straight-laced state trooper was the one for me.

In April, his doubts disappeared, and he proposed. We quickly began planning a huge Victorian wedding for September, to be held in my sister Julie's backyard, despite others saying we were rushing into marriage.

I couldn't believe I had finally found the love I'd been

looking for, and I wanted our lives together to start as soon as possible. After the announcements were mailed out in August, Gary got cold feet again, and though we tried to reconcile, we parted ways. We tried seeing other people, but dating only reinforced to both of us how much we missed each other.

A few days before Thanksgiving, Gary called and told me life was too short to spend it apart. He'd had a change of heart. We were re-engaged on Christmas, and there was only one thing left to do … elope.

It was January, and once again, a snowy day signaled a beautiful moment for me as we headed to Sun River to marry. Preparations were simple. With my hair done, I stepped into the Jessica McClintock dress I'd imagined wearing for our originally planned wedding. This time, I would wear it for Gary's eyes only, and the moment was perfect, knowing we shared it only with each other. This was my fairytale. This was our moment.

In a Sun River church, on a sunny day, my Prince Charming stood ready to marry me dressed in his police uniform. A counselor from Gary's department performed the ceremony, and as we said, "I do," the world came into focus. This was the love I'd been searching for.

We spent our honeymoon riding quads, snow-skiing and playing together like two kids without a care. The stress from our past was gone, and the rest of the world had fallen away. Gary had rescued me.

❧❧❧

Too quickly, cracks began to form in the frame of our fairytale. One week out of every month, Gary traveled to do extra training for work, and he seemed more and more distracted as the days passed. Only eight months of our marriage passed before he told me he wanted to end it.

"Did you have an affair?" I was sure he had.

"No," he assured me, but the thought of an ended marriage was more than I could take. My life scraped bottom. As my dream of a perfect world crumbled around me, the only peace I found was in the decision to end my own life. Every hole I'd struggled to seal inside me had been reopened, and this time there was no closing wounds ripped apart anew. My life proved rejection the only constant, being cast aside the rhythm of my life, and my heart could no longer contain the endless hurt. My husband didn't want me. My own mother didn't want me. The ache inside my chest was unbearable yet again.

The same invisible knife still stuck in my heart since my little girl days, days when chocolate milk and handfuls of aspirin in a school cafeteria seemed the answer. The same chasm of emptiness had widened further still, and the only plausible answer to stop the hurt permanently, to end the pain forever, returned again — death.

This time I chose to take back the only control I had left. I could choose when to leave this world. Every move was calculated. For two weeks, I planned the end of my life in my head while I worked as if everything was normal. I made sure I had an extra bottle of the prescription sleeping pills I had been taking for insomnia.

TOTAL RESTORATION

One night, I went to a bar with a friend from the gym. We drank a couple bottles of wine, and I went home. As I entered the top unit duplex Gary and I lived in, I realized he wasn't home, and I knew this would be the night. I went back downstairs to get the pills out of my car and climbed them again to begin the last night of my life.

In the quiet, I took what I planned to be my last bath. Then, I peacefully prepared my will. As I stared blankly at the paper, I second-guessed myself and shoved the definitive paper under tepid bathwater, waiting for the felt pen ink to run. But the ink didn't run. It wouldn't run, and the words staring up at me solidified the end for me was real. It couldn't be erased.

After each pill found its place inside my body, relief washed over me. I knew once I lay down, it would all be over. My peace came in the form of 40 prescription sleeping pills. My endless chase for love and stability was ending. Now, I could finally rest.

ॐ ॐ ॐ

I woke to find my plan had failed. My mother-in-law had been concerned when she couldn't reach me by phone. An ambulance arrived too late to pump my stomach. The doctors said I should be dead.

My family was angry, wanting to put me in a mental ward. All I could think about was how God allowed me to live when so many others in my situation had not survived. Despite the physical sickness I felt for the next few days while my body tried to recover, I believed God was the one who spared me. I ached with the knowledge that part of me was still dead inside. My marriage was over.

Gary checked me out of the hospital and said, "What do you want to do?"

All I could say is, "I want to go home." And we did go home, but a few short days later, I moved out of the house.

૰૰૰

The hospital insisted I go for counseling, which I needed, but it wasn't enough.

I found myself in church one night with my sister Julie, emotional and upset about all that had happened. The minister, Louis Hernandez, asked for people to come to the front of the church if they wanted to pray, so I went with my sister.

The minister placed his hands upon my head, and I could feel my sister's hands upon me, too. They began to pray for me. A warmth I'd never felt before flooded my body, soothing my insides with an instant peace. Even though others were praying around me, the noise faded away as I experienced an intense connection to God. My heart was being wiped clean, it seemed.

I lit up as a language I didn't know escaped my lips. I felt whole. Hope had found me in a crowded church, and it felt as if God literally wrapped his arms around me. I knew even though I didn't have all I wanted, even though my marriage was still broken, I had God. What he had to give me was better than anything I could find on my own.

When I reached my car, I kept thinking over and over, *Is this for real?* Would my mouth form those strange syllables even in my car, away from the minister, away from the church building? I opened my mouth to test this new language, and it still worked. This new experience did for me what the counseling had not been able to do. It pulled me up out of the darkness I was trapped in.

A lifetime of hurt, disappointment and rejection seemed to empty out of me in that church building, and I knew I needed God more than I needed anything. I couldn't control what anyone else in this world would do or had done. I could only be responsible for myself and what I believed.

Looking over the experiences of my life, I could now see God always had my back through every painful experience, through every longing to die. He never left, and he would never leave. He kept me alive.

❧❧❧

Christmas rolled around, and things between Gary and me changed yet again. He decided he didn't want to live without me. He could see me as his wife. He could see me as the mother of his children. We got back together.

My boss had given me a spa day gift for Christmas, and Gary and I went together. He got the massage I didn't want; I got the facial. While I lay on the table, I heard God speak to me as clearly as if he were standing in the room next to me. *Prepare yourself. The truth will be known to you.*

I braced for bad news, and when we got home, Gary started acting strange. He was drinking water and not being himself. Then, he sat me down and told me. He'd had an affair while we were separated, and I was devastated again because he had lied when I asked him before. The familiar stabbing pain shot through my heart again as I relived the roller coaster of familiar emotions.

Tears ran down my face as I sat in the bathtub thinking over all that had transpired in my marriage, in my life, and I realized even through the pain that I loved him. I loved Gary. I could forgive him. We were meant to be together. God had prepared me only hours before, and I knew I could let the pain go. Forgiveness came, and our marriage was restored.

ॐॐॐ

Our first son, Mark, was born in July of 1991, 26 days early, and though there were some complications during and after the pregnancy, Mark and I survived. Mark spent the first several days of his life in the NICU, but when he was finally released to come home, I was elated. I spent every moment with my little baby. I finally had my own child to nurture and love.

Gary and I stared down at our little Mark and laughed as we asked, "What have we done?" Here was this beautiful child we'd both had a part in creating, and he was perfect. Parenthood was nothing but wonderful.

Two years later, William, our second son, came along, and our family was complete. Gratitude overwhelmed me as I realized I was nothing like my own mother. Though I felt no emotional connection to her, God had allowed me to experience boundless love toward my babies. I needed my children, and they needed me. I could express all of those emotions with my children that I never experienced.

I knew as I looked at my precious babies that my life was not my own. All the wondering was over. I was in love with my boys, and nothing could ever stop the nurturing warmth I felt when I looked at them. These beautiful children were mine. I could live for my children, to see every milestone as they reached it. They would never have to wonder if I was ever coming back because I would never leave.

かかか

I needed to let Gary know I was on my way home from having dinner with my sister and a friend. As I drove around the lake, I reached for my cell phone. My turquoise green Ford Explorer slid on a patch of gravel left over from a recent road-paving construction project. The car bounced down off the road, came back and then slipped off the road again, hitting a cattle guard. I felt the car spin out of control and flip over, again and again, only to stop after crashing into a power pole, which came down hard upon the roof. All the windows smashed out. Live power lines dangled around me, and I found myself under the dashboard in shock.

A neighbor from across the street came to help (my personal guardian angel, as I later called him). He warned me of downed power lines and kept me safe. I couldn't even open the door to get myself out. Still in shock and not understanding the severity of the crash, I called Gary.

"I think you're going to have to come and get me. I'm in the ditch."

Gary came and helped me out of the car, stunned himself at the sight of the banged-up Explorer. An ambulance took me to the hospital, but after x-rays to check for broken bones, I was cleared to go home. I walked away from a totaled car with a sore body and a cut on my ear. I was alive when I shouldn't have survived.

The accident further reminded me, and those closest to me, how fleeting life is. Every day, I drove by that spot. Every day, I remembered God had spared me yet again.

☙☙☙

Twenty-two years after the weekend Gary proposed marriage, we were on our way to a Marriage Encounter, a retreat getaway. Together with three other couples, two on the verge of ending their marriages, we embarked on the task of strengthening our relationships.

Love infused every activity and exercise given to us. Questions were asked, and we were sent to our rooms to write our answers without interruption. As we read each other's words, vulnerable and raw, hurt and misunderstanding melted.

I had no idea about the feelings Gary harbored inside, and he now understood my fears, too. We grew right in front of each other as we wrote and shared and talked through years of hidden thoughts and feelings. In one weekend, we expressed more honesty than in 20 years of marriage. Weights lifted from both our guarded souls as we laid every struggle bare.

At the end of our retreat, the time for vow renewals came, and all four couples participated. Every marriage had undergone strengthening and healing. Words once spoken out of obligation and hopeful anticipation were now spoken freely out of want and desire. We chose each other again knowing the ups and downs in our past and despite the inevitable ups and downs in our future.

The fairytale had its place once upon a time between us, but this time, vows were solidified with the years of reality we'd shared. We were bound spiritually, in tenderness, choosing to say the words instead of being told to repeat them.

Without judgment or impatience, we spilled our hurts and fears in ink, resulting in a deeper level of understanding we'd never been able to achieve. I didn't feel interrogated. He didn't feel appeased. My fear of being rejected again upon sharing my mind and heart was lifted, and we continued the hard work even after we returned home. Problems came in waves, but we'd leaned into the waves our marriage sent, the easy and the hard, and we'd become stronger for it. We expected a nice getaway. What we got was a transformation, a marriage forever changed.

ॐॐॐ

As I looked at the stuffed panda bear in front of me, I remembered the ache of needing and wanting love. Through so many years, I fought with feeling forgotten and abandoned. Now, here I stand with a family I always dreamed about having, as I'd taken care of my little panda. The panda bear has always been a reminder of security for me as I've collected them through the years, but now I know — security is more than a stuffed bear to keep me warm. And even though we get hurt by people when we least expect it, not everyone leaves.

Even if the whole world walked away from me, I'd never be alone. He'd be there. Fall Creek, junior high camp, a stomach full of aspirin and chocolate milk, another stomach full of sleeping pills and a car wrapped around a power pole — God had been there to rescue me again and again and again.

I didn't have to pretend anymore. Not only did I have my marriage and children, but I'd been blessed with a church family at Living Faith Assembly, a church family who never judges or condemns. I never knew how a pastor and his wife could love like Pastor Rulon and Dana have. Through tears and support and prayers, their compassion has lifted us up during some of our darkest times. And love shines through the people at Living Faith, too, as they've come alongside us in our most vulnerable moments.

Survival wasn't what I thought it was. Survival wasn't my ability to white-knuckle my way through life. Survival was outside of me and my panda bears and my aching heart. Survival was love in the form of a God whose hands never stopped holding me through it all. Survival was letting his hands hold me, even through the telling of a story that ached to tell. Survival means knowing God is always there, and if he's always there, I'm never alone.

A FRIEND FOR LIFE
The Story of Kristine
Written by Karen Koczwara

No! No! Stop it! What is happening to me?

A scream emerged from somewhere deep inside my throat as darkness crept in. My husband's face contorted into an evil mask before my eyes, and hands clawed at me from below, trying to pull me toward the floor. My house transformed into a place of terror as I thrashed about hysterically, panicked and out of control.

Another piercing scream followed.

Someone make this nightmare stop!

And then there was only blackness.

ৡৡৡৡ

I was born in 1948 near Beaverton, Oregon. I spent my early days as a tomboy, exploring the rambling countryside with my four brothers. My father held a job operating heavy equipment, while my mother stayed at home with us. We lived in Copper Mountain, a remote area just outside town, where we attended classes in a small three-room schoolhouse. Though I had several acquaintances on the playground, I never made any close friends.

I began my freshman year at the high school in Beaverton. With nearly 2,000 students, the school was a far cry from the tiny one I'd attended outside town. I quickly got lost in the crowd. While the other teenage girls talked of boys and slumber parties, I preferred to stay to myself. I passed the days climbing trees, singing and walking in the woods alone. My parents discouraged me from dating, but on a few occasions, I snuck out to meet up with boys.

Just before graduation, I began dating an older boy. After knowing him for only six months, we decided to get married. We embarked on a two-week honeymoon, but after we returned, he immediately distanced himself. He spent his nights hanging out at the bars, while I worked at a café and a nursing home to pay the bills. We became like two strangers, and eventually, he stopped coming home and disappeared altogether.

Life marched on. I landed a job at a factory and befriended a girl there. She needed a place to stay and moved in with me. Her boyfriend, Jim, often came down from the University of Oregon to visit her. Jim introduced me to pot, and I enjoyed the temporary high after smoking a few joints. I took up smoking cigarettes, too. After my friend and Jim broke up, I continued meeting up with him, and we began dating. He was quick-witted and smart, and I loved his charisma. I officially filed for divorce from my first husband, married Jim in January 1969 and enrolled at the University of Oregon shortly after.

In the '60s, drugs and rock and roll dominated the scene. Long-haired hippies puttered down the street in brightly colored VW vans, waving peace signs and protesting the Vietnam War. Drugs flowed freely, and anyone from teenagers to upper-class folks joined in the flower child party. Jim introduced me to this world, and it quickly sucked me in. As a girl who'd spent much of her childhood alone in the countryside, I enjoyed the way drugs brought me out of my shell. We spent our evenings hopping from one party to the next, snorting or smoking whatever drugs were available. Oftentimes, we didn't know what we popped in our mouths or breathed in, but we were usually too high to care.

One night, while partying at a friend's house, Jim and I took a few hits of the hallucinogenic drug LSD. As we stepped outside to leave, my surroundings immediately grew blurry and terrifying. A large yellow dog rushed out of nowhere and growled at me. I jumped back, terrified as he flashed sharp teeth and lunged. The night sky transformed into a dark, formidable canopy as we headed home.

Back at the house, things grew more surreal. My husband's face, usually cheerful and kind, now twisted into an evil mask, as though he was some sort of demon. The walls appeared to close in as blackness encroached. All of a sudden, it felt as if hands reached out of the floor to grab me. I screamed hysterically as confusion and fear set in, and I lost all control.

What's going on? Where am I? Make this nightmare stop!

The next thing I knew, I woke up in the emergency room of the hospital. I felt like I was floating in space, looking down on the earth, which resembled a tiny blue and white marble. I heard a baby crying off in the distance, and a blinding white light shot before my eyes. The evil darkness was gone, replaced by a strange, peaceful world I could not explain. I tried to utter the word "perfect," but it came out "perrrr."

I have completely left my body. What is happening to me?

I drifted off to sleep, and when I awoke again, I was dressed in a hospital gown and lying in a padded cell. *The psych ward. They put me in here because I was freaking out.* As the grogginess wore off, I suddenly remembered everything — the drugs, the growling dog, the hands trying to pull me into the floor, the way my husband's face had contorted into something evil. I knew without a doubt I had overdosed on LSD and that I was lucky to be alive.

"Well, it looks like you are going to be okay. You can go home soon." A doctor entered the room to check on me.

"I think I might have done something to my toe," I muttered.

"No, you're fine. I checked you out, and I'm going to release you." The doctor seemed especially nonchalant, having no idea of the horror I'd just endured in the last 24 hours. I knew I was just one of the many patients he'd seen who had overdosed in this small college town.

The incident shook me up terribly. When I got home, I asked my husband what exactly had happened.

"You were freaking out and screaming after you

overdosed," he told me. "The neighbors called the police, and an ambulance arrived and took you to the hospital. I followed behind them. The doctors had to give you a downer drug to counteract the LSD."

I shuddered, replaying the events in my mind. I had never been so frightened in my entire life. I did not fully understand the significance of the bright white light and the out-of-body experience in the emergency room, but I did know one thing. I was done with drugs for good.

I began spending time with my lovely sister-in-law, Ann. Ann was unlike anyone I'd ever met. She loved God and often talked about how good he was. A light seemed to shine through her from the inside out. I was intrigued by her kindness and her wisdom, and I grew to love her as a best friend.

"You can have God in your life, too, Kristine," Ann told me. "Would you like to invite him into your heart?"

I hadn't spent a day in church growing up and knew little about God. But I admired Ann and wanted whatever she had. I wanted the peace she talked about. I bowed my head and prayed, inviting God to come into my life. I asked him to forgive me for the wrong things I'd done and to help me make good decisions. Ann explained that if I simply trusted him with my heart, he would guide me through life. When the world did not make sense, I could rely on him. His love was unconditional, and my relationship with him would continue even after I left this earth someday when I went to heaven. At last, I understood true peace. It was not the sort of peace the hippies talked about as they waved their cardboard signs, but an inexplicable peace that came from deep within. I thanked God for sparing my life after my drug overdose. He had a plan for me, and I looked forward to seeing it unfold.

In 1973, I got pregnant. Though I had given up drugs, I still smoked cigarettes heavily. I knew I didn't want to harm my body or my unborn child. I prayed, asking God to please remove the desire from me. Immediately, I felt the addiction leave. It was as if a heaviness I'd been carrying around suddenly floated out of my body and disappeared. I did not experience a single withdrawal symptom or craving for cigarettes from that day on. In 1974, I gave birth to a beautiful, healthy little girl and marveled over the new life.

One night, I experienced an incredible dream. After stepping up into a beautiful room, I saw Jesus. As I glanced around, everything appeared to be blue. I observed amazing treasures everywhere. Jesus led me to a crystal-clear window, where I could see out for miles into the distance. A stunning city spread out before me, complete with hues of blues and white and other brilliant colors of the rainbow. When I awoke, I knew without a doubt that Jesus was real. Whatever lingering doubts I'd had in my mind disappeared.

I gave birth to another little girl, Heather, in 1975. I loved being a mother and watching my daughters grow. Jim continued doing drugs, and his lifestyle put a strain on our relationship. We fought often about his harmful habits, but he refused to change. He became a drug dealer, and his friends drifted in and out of our house to pick up their goods. While at one time I'd joined in the party, the drugs now disgusted me.

"We have kids now, Jim," I told my husband adamantly. "I don't want this stuff around them."

But Jim didn't stop. He grew more secretive about his habits, and we drifted further apart. Even after being thrown in prison for dealing drugs, he went right back to them when he was released. Desperate to save my marriage, I turned to Ann for help. She encouraged me to keep holding on and to pray for my husband. She also suggested I attend church. I tried going a few times with her, but I didn't get much out of what the pastor said or the songs we sang. *Maybe I'll try it someday, but right now it's not really my thing,* I decided, brushing it off.

Jim often used our walk-in closet at home as a work station for his drugs. He laid his cocaine out in lines there and chopped it up with a razor blade. One day, Jim walked into the closet to find our first-grade daughter playing with the cocaine. Furious, he whipped her. When I discovered what had happened, I was beyond horrified, recalling the terrifying night I'd overdosed on drugs.

"You know what, Jim? I've put up with a lot over the years, but this crosses the line!" I screamed at him. "Do you know what could have happened to our daughter if she ate that? I'm done. I'm taking the girls and leaving. I'm not going to deal with this anymore!"

I packed my things, took our two young girls and

moved out of the house. I landed a good job and enjoyed my work. Jim and I remained separated, each of us hurting in our own ways but unsure of how to put the pieces of our life back together. I loved my husband, but I could not risk putting my daughters in danger. I could only hope and pray he would experience a wake-up call as I had and leave his damaging lifestyle for good.

Ann came to my house one day, visibly shaken by a dream she'd just had. "I dreamt that I was in a parking garage on my way to my car when I was attacked by a group of men. They raped me while my son stood by and watched in horror. It was awful, Kristine. It really scared me. I don't know what it all means." Her eyes widened as she recounted the details.

Ann's nightmare followed in the wake of some strange behavior. Though she was a registered nurse, she often traveled for hours to Eugene to see a doctor. She finally confided that the doctors had found lumps in her breasts, and I feared she might have cancer. But she always remained positive, and I continued to admire her faith in God. No matter what life threw her way, Ann always found a way to make good out of it.

And then one horrible day, I got a phone call that changed my life forever.

"Kristine?" It was Ann's husband on the line, and he screamed so hysterically I could hardly understand him. "Ann was killed in a hunting accident today."

My beloved Ann. Killed? Impossible!

My body went numb as my heart sank to the floor.

Surely, there must be some mistake. Surely, he was not talking about my sister-in-law. *No. No. No. Not my best friend.*

Ann's husband relayed the gruesome details the best he could. She had been out hunting with him and his two sons in the woods. They'd spotted a deer alongside the road, and her stepson had hopped out of the car to shoot it. The deer quickly turned and darted away, and her stepson shot into the air. But at that very moment, Ann stepped out of the vehicle and into the path of the bullet. It struck the back of her head, and she collapsed to the ground and died instantly.

Her stepson was so distraught that he immediately turned the gun on himself and stuck it in his mouth. Her husband jumped out and tackled him to the ground before he pulled the trigger. It was a true nightmare, more brutal than a scene in a horror movie. And in an instant, I crumbled.

"I'll tell Jim," I mustered through my sobs.

Somehow, my legs propelled me to the car. In a daze, I drove to Jim's place, still hoping that what I was about to tell him was not true. Ann simply could not be dead. She was my best friend, my absolute rock. I leaned on her for everything. How could God take her from me? Was this some sort of sick joke?

Jim's face lit up when he saw me. "Hi, Kristine! Come on in!" He happily led me inside.

Sick with dread, I followed him in and sat down. The words sounded foreign as they tumbled out of my mouth.

"Your sister has been killed. She was shot in a hunting accident."

Jim stared at me in disbelief. His eyes grew wide with horror as he flew into a rage. "I thought you were gonna tell me that you were moving back in, but all you came over to tell me is that my sister got her brains blown out!"

I sat frozen to my seat, unable to move or speak. *This isn't happening right now. This is a nightmare, just like the one Ann had, and I am going to wake up at any moment, right?*

And then it hit me — the dream Ann had shared with me. In it, her son had watched as she'd been brutally attacked. In real life, it was her son who had killed her. Was it a horrible coincidence? Had it been a vision? No matter what, one thing remained — Ann was not coming back. I had lost her forever.

Jim and I attended Ann's funeral together in Portland. As the pastor shared and her loved ones gathered to grieve, I completely fell to pieces. Instead of her death bringing Jim and me closer, it only drove us further apart. Each time I looked at his face, I saw hers. I could not accept the fact that my best friend was gone. She had been taken from me in a heartbeat, without any warning or goodbye. It was more than a tragedy — it was an unthinkable horror.

Distraught, I decided to take a leave of absence from work. I spent my days down by the river, sobbing until my insides hurt. Grief, doubt, self-pity and selfishness overcame me. Jim and I officially divorced, and I tried to move on with my life. At last, I returned to work, but Ann's death haunted me day and night. I wished more than anything I could rewind time and stop her from stepping out of that car. She had been the glue in my marriage, the one I believed held Jim and me together during our roller coaster relationship. Who would be my confidante and mentor now?

Instead of turning to God, I grew angry with him. He'd allowed a terrible tragedy to occur without stopping it. Perhaps all this stuff Ann had shared with me over the years really wasn't so great after all. If God loved me as much as she said, why did he let me suffer? My marriage had crumbled, and my best friend was gone. I stopped praying to God, turned away from him and picked up alcohol instead. The booze temporarily numbed the pain and helped me get through my long, lonely days.

I threw myself into social activities for the next several years and went to the bars with my co-workers at night. One evening, I met a guy named Bruce at a bar. Though 10 years my junior, he took a special interest in me. We began dating, and I appreciated his companionship. Bruce made it clear that he enjoyed making and spending money. He was impressed with my good-paying job. He also enjoyed drinking. Just as Jim had whisked me into the world of drugs, Bruce pulled me further into the world of alcohol. It was now the mid-80s, and pop-rock and hairspray now dominated as the hippie days faded away. My new lifestyle seemed perfectly acceptable, but I had no idea of the difficult days that lay ahead.

TOTAL RESTORATION

Bruce and I married in June 1986. We bought a large, beautiful house in the Eugene area and settled in with my two daughters, both now teenagers. Bruce landed a job as a lumber broker, and my company promoted me. We took multiple lavish vacations to Hawaii, the Cook Islands and Florida Keys. For a while, life seemed nearly idyllic. On the outside, I had everything a girl could want — a young, handsome husband, a gorgeous home and an extravagant lifestyle. I shoved the pain of my past aside, along with my relationship with God.

And then, in a string of horrible events, our picture-perfect life fell to pieces. I discovered Bruce was having an affair, and I was devastated. I tried to forgive him, but I was already scarred from my reckless relationship with Jim. *I don't know if I can go through this again. It's too painful.* I went numb instead, going through the motions of life as a shell of a person.

One day, I came home to find a note. It was from an employee at Child Protective Services. "I have your daughter Noelle. She has been placed in foster care, and until further investigation, you will not be able to see her."

No! There must be some terrible mistake! Foster care? What on earth is going on?

I immediately went to the authorities, who informed me that 15-year-old Noelle had indeed been placed in foster care after CPS removed her from our home. Noelle had come forward with allegations that my husband had abused her. Just like the day I learned of Ann's death, I completely fell to pieces. Was this all true? How could it have gone on under my own roof without me noticing? Sickened, I confronted Bruce, but he denied everything.

"I don't know what you are talking about," Bruce said coolly, looking me straight in the eye. "She must be making stuff up, Kristine."

I'd trusted Bruce when I married him, but he'd already proven to be dishonest. Could I really believe him when he said he hadn't touched my daughter?

The nightmare continued as the police and social services followed through with a thorough investigation. I remained focused on one thing — getting my daughter back home safe. Her case went to trial, and Bruce was found not guilty. She returned home, scarred and badly shaken by the ordeal. We cried together as she shared the gruesome details. She insisted Bruce had abused her. I took three weeks off of work, and the two of us took a vacation together to hash everything out. I felt I had somehow failed her because I had not protected her. I also worried for my other daughter. Had Bruce touched her, too? One thing was certain — I was done with Bruce. I had to get out of this marriage.

Just when I thought I'd experienced all the shock my heart could take, another bombshell dropped. I learned a financial company was suing Bruce for embezzling thousands of dollars from the lumber company where he worked. He was in serious trouble.

"Is this true?" I demanded of Bruce. "You better tell me what's going on!"

But Bruce kept his cool. "I have no clue about any of

that," he said, shrugging his shoulders. "There must be some sort of mistake."

"I don't believe you," I hissed. "We're done, Bruce. I'm leaving. You can keep the house, but I'm taking the girls. This marriage is over."

I've married a con man. I'm on the brink of my third divorce. What have I done? Disgusted, I packed my things and moved the girls into an apartment. Within no time, Bruce fell behind on the house payments, and the place went into foreclosure. The big, beautiful house, the expensive trips, the romance — it all had been a sham. I'd been duped by a man who had lied to my face and nearly ruined my life. What could possibly happen next?

I spent the next couple years attempting to rebuild my life. I was grateful for a good job that paid the bills. I focused on the girls and work, and in the evenings, I went out to the bars and had a few drinks. The booze continued to numb the pain, and I enjoyed socializing with the regulars who came in. Deep down, I sensed a lingering emptiness. I needed something meaningful — something more than just a few beers and a good time. But I was not ready to address my wounds just yet.

The company I worked for went belly up. I found a new job, and I enjoyed my duties, but I was also lonely and ready for a new relationship. I wondered if there were any good men left out there and if I could ever trust my heart to anyone again.

One day, my daughter told me she'd met the perfect guy for me. "His name is Bill, and he comes into the bar where I waitress," she told me. "He's a bit older, but he's really sweet. He brings vegetables from his garden for us sometimes. I think you should meet him."

I agreed to meet Bill, and we hit it off. He was kind and seemed liked a genuine guy. We began dating, and in August 2000, we married. Bill was a drinker, but it didn't bother me, as I was, too. I quit my job, and Bill retired from his work as a carpenter when he turned 62. But not long after, the doctors diagnosed him with prostate cancer. I'd now lost all my health benefits with work, and we knew the benefits Bill got through Medicare would not cover his treatment. I decided I'd better find some sort of employment again.

Not wanting a full-time, stressful job, I secured work as a cook for the school district. From 6 a.m. to 1 p.m. every day, I prepared a variety of hot meals for hundreds of hungry students. It wasn't an especially glamorous job, but the benefits helped pay for Bill's radiation treatments. The doctors eventually gave him a clean bill of health, though he still checked in with them on a regular basis to get tested. His diabetes remained troublesome, but I was grateful he was cancer-free.

With the girls now grown and moving on with their lives, it was time to focus on mine. Bill and I continued to drink regularly. Every night, I went into the kitchen and poured us a few drinks before bed. Alcohol had been such a regular part of my life over the prior few years that I hardly thought twice about cracking open the bottle. *I am okay,* I convinced myself. *My life is pretty good. Things haven't been easy, but they could be worse. My husband is healthy, the girls are doing well and we have everything we need.* But that notion couldn't have been further from the truth. I didn't have everything I needed. In fact, I was missing out on the most important thing on earth.

One sunny day in July 2011, I stood at my kitchen window, looking outside at my beautiful yard. I usually loved summertime, as it offered endless opportunities to spend time in the green outdoors. But on this particular day, I felt anything but happy. Even the gorgeous sunshine could not lure me outside. All alone in the house, it hit me with full force — *I am depressed. My life is empty. There is nothing left anymore. The girls are gone, my career is over and, while I have Bill, I don't have many meaningful relationships. Is this how life looks when you get older — just a purposeless, mundane existence?*

Just then, the phone rang. It was my daughter on the line.

"Mom, I don't know what life is about anymore. I am so depressed. I don't think I believe in God anymore. I don't know what to do." She sounded distraught.

Her words hit me with force. My daughter had struggled over the past few years, making destructive choices as I had. I scrambled to find the words to encourage her, but I couldn't come up with much. After all, her thoughts mirrored mine. How could I explain to my daughter that I wasn't sure there was much meaning to life, either? What sort of example had I set for her?

After I hung up the phone, I glanced again out the

window, where the sun danced on the trees just a few feet away. Suddenly, I knew what I needed to do. I recognized what I'd been missing all these years — God. I had invited him into my life years before, but I'd pushed him away after Ann's death, convinced he didn't care. I'd been angry, confused, bitter and heartbroken. I'd tried doing things my way, but it hadn't worked out very well. With a string of failed marriages behind me, it occurred to me that I'd been looking for love and affection in all the wrong places. God was the only one I'd needed all along. I thought about the dream I'd had years before, when he'd shown me the beautiful city. I'd known he was real all along, but I'd pretended I didn't need him. I only hoped it wasn't too late for him to hear my desperate prayers.

I dropped to my knees and began to cry. "God, please forgive me. I know I've made so many mistakes and turned my back against you. I promise you, though; I am never leaving you again. I will follow you for the rest of my days, if you will have me back."

Through my tears, I sensed God's presence, right there with me, as though he'd never left at all. And then it hit me. He had never left. I had been the one to walk away, but he had never given up on me. He still loved me, and he was welcoming me back into his arms at this very moment. The warm and peaceful feeling I'd once felt after inviting him into my life instantly returned, and I thanked him for giving me a second chance. It was a moment of pure celebration. I was home again.

It felt wonderful to talk to God again. It was like we

were long-lost friends and had much to catch up on. I shared my heart with him and began listening to him. As I did, he filled in the details of that horrific night when I'd overdosed on drugs. I realized that when I was in the emergency room, I'd been looking down on Jesus. I had seen his perfect love, and I'd tried to mutter "Perfect," but the word had not quite come out. I had not known Jesus then, but he still saved my life. Even during my darkest hour, he pursued me.

What's next, God? What do I do now? I prayed.

Find your spiritual family, or you will fall away from me again, I felt God whisper.

He was right. It was time for me to go to church. I had not set foot in a church in years, as it had not seemed very important. But I now understood why Ann talked about it so much. Life was not meant to be lived alone. It was meant to be shared with others. I had tried doing life by myself, but it had only proven empty. I needed to be around people who loved God and who loved me, too.

I grabbed the phonebook and flipped through it to locate a church in the Cottage Grove area. I stumbled onto Living Faith Assembly in Cottage Grove. *That sounds nice,* I thought. *I'll give it a try on Sunday.*

The moment I walked through the doors of the church, I felt welcomed and cared for. The people were warm and friendly as they introduced themselves. The pastor shared about God's love, reminding us that if we trusted in him, we could experience peace in our lives. *This is what I've been missing,* I confirmed. *I need to be here. This is where I belong. I know I still have much healing to do, but this is definitely a step in the right direction.*

I knew I needed to give up drinking alcohol. I prayed, asking God for strength. Immediately, he took all desires from me. I did not experience a single withdrawal symptom. I thanked him for removing something that had controlled my life for so many years. The alcohol seemed harmless at the time, but I recognized that I'd been using it to numb my pain. While it offered a temporary escape, it only left me feeling emptier in the morning. Now that I had God and a new church, I did not need to turn to booze anymore. I had found true fulfillment.

Bill continued to drink, and each night, I poured him his usual concoction before bed. I began pouring myself a soda instead so I had something to sip on as well. One evening, however, as I popped open my soda can, a little voice inside whispered, "Just one drink can't hurt. You can still be a Christian and have a drink. If you don't drink, Bill will never come to God."

I recognized this voice as a dangerous one that wanted to undermine my better intentions. This dark voice wanted to tempt me and lure me back into my old lifestyle. I considered it for a moment as I glanced back and forth from the soda pop to the bottle of booze. *This is it, Kristine. You can choose right now. Are you going to give in and have a drink?*

But then I heard another voice, and I knew it was from God. He reminded me that I was his. I didn't need to pick up that booze because he had delivered me from it. *I set you free from that, Kristine,* he whispered. I took a deep breath and kept pouring the soda, thanking God for helping me to make the right choice. I knew other temptations would come my way. I imagined the devil himself might try all sorts of tricks to get me to take my eyes off God and make bad choices. This was why it was so important to stay in church and keep focused on God. He was my strength.

I became more involved in Living Faith Assembly and enjoyed the teaching and the new friendships I made. I volunteered to cook meals for the youth group, got plugged in with the women's group and sometimes ran the Jumbo-Tron on Sunday mornings. I often invited Bill to go with me, but he politely declined. Bill had been raised in a Baptist church but had had a disturbing church experience in his later years. He'd quit going altogether and hadn't had much interest since. I loved Bill and continued to pray for him, hoping he'd change his mind and decide to join me one day. After all, there'd been a time when I didn't want much to do with church, either. But God had opened my heart, and now I couldn't imagine not going.

Summer turned to fall. The Oregon air grew crisp, and the leaves on the trees turned brilliant hues of orange and red. One evening, as I slept peacefully on the couch, I heard a gentle but very clear voice next to me. *It is I, the Messiah. Welcome.* When I opened my eyes, I didn't see anyone there, but I knew Jesus had come to visit me. He was present in the room with me, and he'd come to let me know what his voice sounded like. I made a commitment in my heart to pay attention to that voice and grow in my relationship with God from then on.

As I continued to read my Bible, attend church and pray, I learned that I could hear God's voice if I truly listened. Sometimes it would come as a soft whisper, other times it might come as a nudging in my heart. If I was really in tune with him, I would be able to decipher his voice from the others in my mind, just as I had the night I'd been tempted to drink again. That voice was what I learned to call the Holy Spirit.

One December evening that year, I spent some time reading my Bible and then decided to make a dessert for Bill. Just before I popped it in the oven, I heard God say to me, *You are going to burn yourself.* I recognized his voice and opted for a bigger potholder. But as I slipped the dessert into the oven, I burnt my pinky finger and yelped in pain. *Whoa! He was right!*

I went back to reading my Bible and began poring through the book of Genesis. In it, I read many stories of men and women just like me. Some had chosen to obey God, but others had decided to make bad choices, and they'd suffered the consequences. *If you listen and obey my words, you will not suffer,* I felt God say to me. As he did, he completely lifted the pain out of my finger. Suddenly, it felt as good as new.

I am going to obey you from now on, God! I told him emphatically. And I meant it.

TOTAL RESTORATION

I'd spent years making bad choices that resulted in painful consequences. *If I'd just followed you, God, I could have avoided so much heartache. Help me to always listen to your voice first.*

The following year, as I raked my front yard one day, I decided to take a break and sit down. Tired and dirty, I plopped myself onto the porch for a few moments. Suddenly, I felt God whisper, *Look to me.* I closed my eyes, and as I did, I experienced a wonderful, inexplicable feeling. It was as if our two hearts were joining and becoming one, right there on my front porch. I had never felt so close to God, and I wondered why I'd ever left him at all. I had missed out on so much joy! But it was not too late. I had the rest of my life and then eternity to spend time with him.

A couple weeks later, God spoke to me again. *Remember the story of Peter in the boat?* I closed my eyes and pictured it.

In the Bible, I'd read about one of Jesus' friends, Peter. One day, Jesus had asked Peter to walk toward him on the water. But Peter doubted Jesus, and as he took his eyes off of him, he started to sink. When he kept his eyes on Jesus, however, he stayed afloat. *The water is the waves of the world,* God told me. *It is the bitterness you held inside. But if you keep your eyes on Jesus, you can rise above all that.*

I loved the lesson God showed me that day. I just needed to keep my eyes on him and not look down, and then I would be okay.

A FRIEND FOR LIFE

"Mom, I've been doing a lot of thinking and praying," my daughter said when she called me one day. "I've seen how God has turned your life around, and I want him to do the same thing in me."

I was thrilled. I'd prayed for my daughter often, knowing she'd endured much pain over the years. Jesus was the only true peace and hope, and it gave me great joy to know God had brought her full circle.

God continued to teach me things over the next year. I felt like an eager student just starting school, ready to learn and grow. One night, I experienced something especially significant. While sleeping, I felt someone's arm around me as he gently woke me up. The feeling was comforting and made me feel safe. In my groggy state, I wondered if it was Bill or perhaps even the dog, but I then realized it was God. He had pulled me into a loving embrace in the middle of the night just to show me how much he loved me. I relaxed into the hug and let him hold me, like a child gives in to a mother's tenderness. As I did, the fears I'd been struggling with over the years slowly slipped away. Fear had held me in its grip for most of my life. But as I submitted to the hug, those fears were lifted from me and replaced with a peace in my heart. I happily drifted back to sleep. The next morning when I awoke, I wrote about the experience in my journal so I would never forget it.

I had many more dreams during the next few months. I paid attention to them all, trying to listen to the voice of God to see what he might be showing me. One night, I dreamt that I was outside at the bottom of a large rock wall. I was so strong that I could detach rocks from the wall. As I yanked them off, one by one, a crowd of onlookers gathered, impressed by my feat. Suddenly, God appeared. He picked up a large rock and threw it my way. My onlookers became disgusted with me and walked off. When I awoke from the dream, I sat in bed shaken, struggling to piece it together.

What does this mean, God? I know there is some significance.

As I prayed, God showed me what it meant. The rocks represented Jesus, the cornerstone in my life. The onlookers were people who did not know him. God was reminding me to keep my eyes focused on Jesus, instead of getting wrapped up impressing people with Bible knowledge or ministry. While those were all good things, he wanted to let me know to follow him — not his teaching. If I simply did that, I would be okay, just like Peter who'd walked on the water.

My dreams began to wane, but I continued to listen to God's still, small voice. In November 2012, I had just gone to bed when I suddenly felt sick, as though I might throw up. I let out a deep groan, and as I did, I felt like I was being lifted off the bed by some sort of powerful force of energy. I knew I was awake, but I didn't want to open my eyes. I had never felt anything like it in my entire life. When at last I opened my eyes, I didn't see anyone there, but I knew what I'd felt, and it felt real. I interpreted the experience as further evidence that God was with me, reminding me once again that there was a battle raging for my heart. The devil wanted to tempt me in any way he could and draw my eyes away from God, but God was more powerful. He was my protector and the only one I needed to obey.

అ అ అ

It was a beautiful summer day in Cottage Grove, Oregon, the type of day that made tourists want to stay forever. I glanced around my acre of land, breathing in the beauty around me. My life had begun in the country as a young girl, and I'd often found comfort in exploring the countryside. Today, as a 64-year-old woman, I still enjoyed the outdoors. Bill, an avid gardener, often rose at 4 a.m. to work on our large garden, and I enjoyed the fruits of his labor. *Our own little slice of paradise,* I marveled.

My big yellow Labrador dog bounded up to me, and I patted him playfully on the head. My mind drifted to that terrible night after I'd overdosed on LSD, when I'd been so frightened by that big yellow dog. I never dreamed I'd own an identical dog. My furry friend represented just one more way God had brought my life full circle since I'd given my heart back to him.

Each day, I thanked God for restoring my life. I wasted years not listening to his voice as I chose to walk my own path. But I now realized that his path was best. Jim had not been so fortunate. He'd finally succumbed to a destructive lifestyle of drug abuse when, at the age of 55, he passed away. He still held a special place in my heart, and I was saddened that he'd never found his way. I'd been headed down that destructive road as well, but God had rescued me from it and restored my hope. My life today held purpose because I lived for him.

I'd tried running from God, but he never gave up on me. Just as my favorite Bible verse reads in Romans 8:38-39, "For I am convinced that neither life nor death, neither angels nor demons, neither the present nor the future, nor any power, neither height nor depth, nor anything else in creation, will be able to separate us from the love of God that is in Christ Jesus our Lord," I knew that nothing could separate me from God's love. I took great comfort in knowing he had a plan for my life. He continued to remind me of his presence in big and little ways, from his beautiful creation in my own backyard to his still, small voice in my heart.

As I headed back inside, I took one last long breath of the fresh summer air. Fall would come soon enough, bringing with it another crop of colorful leaves. Next would come winter, ushered in by cloudy skies and chilly rain. But spring would poke its way through after that, and as the buds would blossom on the trees, life would reveal itself again.

Just like the Oregon countryside, my life had cycled through many seasons as well. Some had been unbearably painful, some truly joyous. I'd grieved and I'd laughed, and in the midst of it all, I'd found true healing and hope.

A FRIEND FOR LIFE

There would be more challenges, but I would not face them alone. I had Jesus now. Ann had been a true friend, and I still missed her terribly. But Jesus was my friend for life, and I would never walk away from him again.

FOREVER AND ALWAYS
The Story of Gary and Sherrie Cooper
Written by Miranda Koerner

"He's not going to make it."

"He's going to make it," a second voice argued. My ears pricked up. I knew that voice. Smooth as glass and soft as cotton but as firm as steel, it was a voice that would not be argued with. I commanded my eyes to lift, but they were like cement. All I could do was listen.

"Ma'am, your husband's vitals and stats are terrible. Continuing to medically resuscitate over and over isn't worth it. I really think you should call in family to say their goodbyes."

"It's not his time."

"Pardon me, ma'am, but you're not a doctor. I am."

"That doesn't mean you're not wrong," the woman repeated.

The hushed voices floated around me. Finally succeeding in cracking my eyes open, a determined smile greeted me in a haze of white.

An angel gazed down at me with love, but I could see the fear in her eyes. In the glare of the hospital lights, her hair shimmered like a halo, and her cheeks pinked with anger.

"You don't know what a fighter my husband is." She reached down and locked her fingers through mine. "He's been to the door of hell. This isn't anything we can't get through."

I tried to speak, but my tongue lay useless, and my stone lips couldn't part. I squeezed back. The doctor mumbled something under his breath and made his escape. Sitting on the bed, Sherrie leaned over and pressed her forehead to my chest. Her tears soaked my hospital gown.

"Please, God." Her whispered prayer echoed like a shout. "Please, God, don't take him home yet. Don't take him from me."

I'm just thankful God heard her prayer.

෨෨෨

It all started with a bang. In the slick '70s as a flashy businessman working at a Buick dealership, I knew the second I saw Sherrie in the office that I wanted her to be mine. With her legs that went on for days and luscious brunette locks, she was the object of every man's dream. At first, she rebuffed my advances because she mistakenly heard I was a married man. As soon as she found out I was single, she agreed to go on a date with me. Two weeks later, we were in love, and within two years, she became Mrs. Gary Cooper, wife and stepmother to my son Craig. She was 21 and I was 36, but that didn't matter to us. All that mattered was being together.

I was raised by a single mother and taught early on that money and luxury were the most important things in life. There was no limit to what I felt I could attain. The more I had, the more I wanted. On my desk, a sign read, "Everyone is dispensable." People thought it was a joke, but it wasn't. All that mattered to me was the bottom line and the amount in my bank account.

I wanted my new wife to live in the lap of luxury — and for all of my friends to envy her. I built her a dream home and bought her favorite car, a Camaro, for our first Valentine's Day together and planned trips for birthdays and big events.

In 1977, soon after we were married, we moved from Sacramento, California, to Ashland, Oregon, and I started working at a dealership, while Sherrie took an administrative job at a nursing home. Times were good, money was flush and we went out, buying nice things and having a good time.

But as they say, all that glitters is not gold.

The pain started at work. Staring at some paperwork, I stifled a gasp. The bottoms of my feet exploded with pain, like a thousand hot needles stabbing over and over.

"Are you okay?" a co-worker asked.

"I'm fine," I lied, clenching my teeth and trying not to double over. I toughed it out through work, and Sherrie and I drove to the doctor's office the next day. He was a specialist in Oregon, who worked in a cold, dark basement office without a hint of warmth. It was a perfect room for the reticent physician, who barely glanced up as I hobbled across his floor.

"It's MS," he grunted.

"How do you know that?" Sherrie burst out. "You haven't even examined him."

He glanced at her and rolled his eyes. Pointing to an examining table, he waited for me to sit.

"I think it's a pinched nerve," I grunted, groaning as the doctor pressed against my foot. "All I need is a pill — ow!"

"Gary, you have nerve pain. Nerve pain and damage is a sign of MS."

I shook my head. I was diagnosed with MS 10 years ago, but ignored it because I didn't feel sick. I was in denial and never told Sherrie. Sherrie was now pregnant with our first child together. We'd only been married three years.

There was so much to do, so much to plan, so much living left. I didn't have time for a disease. "I think I'm just getting older, Doc."

"Gary, MS isn't something you want to mess with." He reached for his prescription pad and scrawled something unintelligible across it. "Let me give you something for the pain."

"Fine, fine." I tried to stifle a yawn.

The doctor caught it and raised an eyebrow. "Have you felt more fatigued lately?"

"Doc, I just turned 40! Of course I'm more tired than usual."

"Fatigue is a sign of MS." He watched me steadily.

"It can't be MS," Sherrie argued. "I've seen patients at the nursing home with MS. They —" She broke off, tears in her eyes. "Oh, honey," she finished, her voice shaky. "This can't be happening."

"I'm sorry." The doctor tore the page off the pad. He held it out, and his eyes met mine. In the icy grey depths lay sympathy that I didn't want to see from anyone, especially him. His gruff words caught me off guard. "Live your life every single day — it can end tomorrow for any of us."

Sherrie took the prescription and shoved it into her purse. "We'll get a second opinion," she said icily.

For the first time, a flicker of emotion passed over the doctor's face. "Wasn't that why you came to see me?"

We rode up the elevator together in silence and walked through the musty waiting room, as dank and dark as the doctor's lair underneath. I reached for Sherrie's hand but didn't take it. I didn't feel I had a right. We walked out together, each of us feeling totally alone.

I didn't want the doctor to be right. I didn't want the pain in my feet to be MS, the never-ending exhaustion, no matter how much sleep I got. But in just a few years, I got to the point where I could barely work. My wife had just welcomed our third son.

What was I going to do? I felt dispensable now.

❧❧❧

The day I found out Gary had kept his MS diagnosis a secret, I had no idea what to think. My first reaction was to throw my arms around him. My second reaction was to feel betrayed. "When were you going to tell me?" I asked him later.

"I'm sorry." He buried his face in his hands. "They told me 10 years ago shortly after I was discharged from the service, but I didn't think it'd come so fast. I was scared you wouldn't marry me." Pride and pain strained his strong jaw. "If you want to leave, I understand."

I could have clocked him. "I'm not going to leave. I would never leave you." Pressing his hand against the swell of my pregnant belly, I looked him straight in the eye. "We're family, Gary. Family doesn't leave. We'll get through this together. I would have married you, even if I knew." He turned, his chin wobbling, and I could tell he didn't want me to see him cry. "Forever and always, right?"

His reply was a hoarse whisper. "Right."

If only I had known how bad it was going to get.

As Gary's pain worsened, the doctors put him on 100 mg of Prednisone, which I began to think of as a drug straight from the devil. That one little pill turned my sweet, loving husband into an angry man determined to control everything and everyone around him. His anger pushed against our love, trying to shove me away, but I held on. Later we discovered that the drug has neurological side effects and can change a patient's personality, but at that time, all I could do was pray he would come back to me. It didn't help that we had our second son, and Gary was no longer able to work. His role as the provider and protector of the family had shifted to me — a hard pill for him to swallow. He tried the Amway business, something he could do without the strain of a full-time job that made him feel he was still contributing. Whenever he met with consultants, he departed excited, only to return frustrated.

"All they did was talk about Jesus," he grumbled, collapsing in his favorite chair. By this time, he required a wheelchair most of the time, and he tired easily. "I went out there for business tips, not to be saved."

I glanced up from the pot I was stirring. "Vicky invited us to a healing service with her. I think it'd be fun." We had been attending church at her invitation for six months, but a healing service was something new.

"Sure. Healing sounds good."

I stirred faster, hoping he wouldn't change his mind. "She told me that if we pray, Jesus might heal you."

He turned on the television, but his chin swiveled my direction. "And how might that happen?"

"A healing service is where everyone prays over you. She said she's seen miracles happen."

Gary's once strong fingers smoothed over his knee and legs. "It'd take a miracle to heal me."

I stopped stirring and held my breath. "So you'll go?"

"I'll go." He turned the channel.

Behind him, I did a silent little dance and then resumed stirring. The last thing I wanted was for him to change his mind. Besides Craig, we had two little boys now, Nick and Chris. I knew I shouldn't, but I was so excited, I told our sons. "When the service is done tonight, Daddy's going to walk down the stairs to pick you up from your classroom," I cooed, wrapping them in their coats. "Jesus is going to heal Daddy."

They clapped their hands and babbled, happy just to see their daddy, let alone see him walking down stairs. During the service, the pastor asked people to come forward.

"Let us heal you, son." He held out his hand, and Gary slid out of his wheelchair and knelt on the floor. People gathered around him, holding hands, touching Gary's back, whispering into his ear. He glanced up, and I cut through the crowd, kneeling next to him and taking his hand.

"Dear God," the pastor began. "Please heal your broken son. Please take this disease from his body, and make him strong again. Make his legs able to run, his breath come easily and his body healthy again."

Gary lifted his chin toward the stained-glass window at the front of the church, as though angels might come pouring out and healing light stream down to him. But there was nothing.

After a few moments, he slowly climbed back in his chair and wheeled out of church. I walked beside him, wrapping my arms around myself and squeezing, trying to stop the tears.

"It's okay, Gary. We can try again. Vicky said —"

He cut me off. "I'm not going to try again."

"But Gary —"

"I think God's got better things to do than heal me." His voice cracked.

I squeezed his shoulder. "I told Nick and Chris you'd be healed," I whispered. "They'll be so disappointed their daddy isn't walking."

For a long moment, Gary didn't say anything. "Maybe God needs to heal my heart first."

If only he knew how right he was.

~~~~

The car was packed, the Christmas presents were wrapped and the kids were bundled into their car seats. "Gary!" I called. "We're ready!"

Even as he locked up the house, I sensed the black cloud brewing around him. I started to ask if he had checked the pipes and turned off the heat, but one look at his stormy brow and I bit my tongue. We got into the car silently, and he pulled out of the driveway and down the road. Gary couldn't walk very well, but he could still drive, an independence he wouldn't relinquish. A little ways down the road, I noticed Gary wasn't stopping to turn into the Chevron we normally filled up at.

"Gary, don't we need gas?" I said gently.

He slammed on the brakes, rocking our sons in their car seats. "Sherrie, do you think I don't know if we need gas? I've been driving 16 years longer than you have!"

"Gary, I just —"

"Forget it! We're not going to see your parents!" He

pulled to the left turn lane and did a U-turn, speeding back to the house. "You can't tell me what to do," he ranted, the speedometer creeping higher. "You're not the boss of me."

Tears welled in my eyes, but I pressed my lips together and didn't say a word. Gary pulled into our driveway and hobbled out, shuffling to the garage door with his cane. I waited until the garage door closed behind him and slid into the driver's seat. By the time I made it down the driveway, the garage door started to open.

"Where's Daddy?" Nick asked from the back. I smiled at him in the rearview mirror, holding back the tears as only a mother can for her child.

"Daddy's going to spend Christmas with his mama. We're going to Grandma and Grandpa's!"

"Yeah!" Nick cheered, and Chris clapped his pudgy baby hands together. I turned on Christmas carols and led the boys in a sing-along, driving the five-hour drive to my parents. After I unloaded the boys and our suitcases, my parents' phone rang. Even before I answered, I knew who it was.

"Hello?"

"If you don't get back here right this instant —"

"Oh, honey, how sweet!" I smiled at my mother, and she smiled back. "Have a wonderful Christmas, too! We'll see you soon!" I hung up the phone. Swallowing the urge to cry, I drank in my sons' smiles. My mom sidled up to me and put a hand on my arm.

"How's he doing?"

"He's … okay. It's hard, Mom." I patted her hand. "I can't thank you and Dad enough for your support."

"Anything you and the boys need, we'll be happy to help." Worry lines crinkled around her eyes. "I just worry about you sometimes."

"MS is a hard disease." I blinked back the tears, refusing to let them come. "It takes everything from you — your nerves, your bowels, your speech, even your eyes and hands. You can't hold anything, can't see anything. It doesn't all come at once, and he's okay so far, but it seems like every time we turn around, there's something else." I watched Nick hand Chris a toy ball, and my lips trembled. "I just hope they get to know their father as he was, before the disease eats him away."

My mom kissed my forehead. "They will," she answered.

ॐॐॐ

When Sherrie walked out on me at Christmas, I thought she'd be back in an hour or two. After dusk had fallen, I called her. I knew she wasn't coming back. I threw the flowers and candy I bought from the corner store — an easy distance with the help of a neighbor — in the trash and stormed back into the house, ranting and raving like a lunatic. Luckily, only the toaster could hear me.

An hour later, the doorbell rang. I opened it and snarled. "What?"

Mario, a friend from the Bible study the church men

encouraged me to attend, raised his hands. "Whoa. You okay?"

"I'm fine. What do you want?" I was rude, but I didn't care. My life was spinning out of control. My wife was working, now she had the car and the checkbook and was at her parents' with the kids. All I could do was sit here and stew.

"I just came by to bring the notes for next week's class." He handed me a sheaf of papers. "Are you sure you're okay?" His eyes darted to the trash can, where flower stems poked out.

I sighed. "I had a fight with Sherrie. She went to her parents for Christmas without me."

He leaned against the doorframe. "Why?"

"Because she's a —" The angry words flamed out on my tongue. I couldn't say such terrible things about my wife.

Mario patted my shoulder. "You know, I lost my family. It's my biggest regret. If I were you, I'd quit being so angry and try to get your family back."

I stared at the flowers in the garbage and nodded. "You're right."

Even though I asked Christ into my heart at church, I didn't really change, at first. Sherrie helped provide, but money was tight. We were never in debt, but I was no longer flashing cash like I used to in my younger days. To our delight, the VA contacted us to let us know veterans with MS were eligible for benefits and financial assistance. Maybe God was answering some prayers after all. I was growing weaker and would soon move to an electric wheelchair, instead of the occasional one. Sherrie, bless her, did it all. Between caring for our sons and working, she was also active in the church, a room mother at school and a full-time caregiver to me.

The next diagnosis nearly did me in. For a while, I silently suffered with jaw pain and had trouble eating, let alone speaking or smiling. The pain was a cross between a branding iron and electric shocks in the side of my mouth. The doctor called it a "suicide disease," since so many people contemplated ending the pain.

Fortunately, I had begun to be a praying man. After seven years of searing pain, the doctor finally had an answer and solution for me.

"It's Trigeminal Neuralgia," the doctor said. "We have a new technique. We can use a laser to burn the nerves in your face to stop the pain."

At that point, I would have tried anything. "We'll pray about it," I said. "Anything is better than surgery."

You know what they say — make plans and God laughs.

☙☙☙

"I don't think he's going to make it."

I froze, about to round the corner to the hallway where Gary was. We were in Oregon, where Gary had been hospitalized for his Trigeminal Neuralgia for a month. I had taken a quick break to run down to the cafeteria to get a cup of coffee and stretch my legs. Two nurses were talking in the hall in hushed voices. I tried not to listen, but their whispers echoed around the tile.

"I don't think her husband will make it through the night."

My heart clenched. *That poor family. I need to pray for them.*

"Can you tell Mrs. Cooper the news?"

I gripped the plastic cup tighter. Not Gary. Not my husband.

The first nurse checked her watch. "Visiting hours are over, anyway. I'll tell her."

"Tell me what?" I rounded the corner. There was no point in hiding anymore.

One nurse recovered first and smoothed her expression into the same calm face she used for every patient. "Your husband is fading, Mrs. Cooper. You need to leave now."

"But you don't think he'll make it through the night, and I have to leave?"

The first nurse nodded. "We're sorry."

"I'm not leaving my husband to die alone."

The second nurse tried to herd me toward the doors. "Mrs. Cooper, visiting hours are over. I'm sorry but—"

"I'm not leaving."

The first nurse glanced at the other. "Do we need to call security? Or are you going to leave? This is a men's ward. Women aren't allowed overnight."

"I will be back in the morning. My husband will make it through the night. And I'll take this up with the administration tomorrow." I tossed my untouched coffee in the trash and turned on my heel, pulling out my cell phone before I reached the doors. I punched in a number I knew by heart, and my pastor answered after two rings.

"Pastor, I need your help. We need to pray for Gary tonight." I left thinking, *I* will *be back tomorrow. He will be okay. I have the power of God behind me.*

Instead of sleeping, I spent the whole night praying, along with most of our church. When I arrived at the hospital the next morning, before I even had a chance to talk to the administrator, a chair waited for me, and Gary had been moved to the window. It was all I could do not to giggle when Gary's surgeon informed the two surly nurses, "Mrs. Cooper will be staying nights with her husband." I was overwhelmed with joy. *Thank you, God.*

I settled into the chair, bumping my arm against a bucket of water on the table next to the bed. I wondered at the tube hanging from the container, but focused my attention on my husband. Later that morning, poor Gary, frozen with agony, followed me with his eyes. Though he wasn't physically paralyzed, the extreme pain made him unable to move. I looked at him and frowned. "He's not breathing right."

The second nurse rolled her eyes. "Like you know how he breathes."

"When you take care of someone for 17 years, you know how he breathes. Please go get a doctor."

The nurse rolled her eyes again and left. I repeated my request for hours, finally getting Gary an x-ray when night was falling. Another hour later, at nearly midnight, the doctor came rushing into the room with a huge syringe in his hand.

"Help me get him up," he ordered, and I obeyed, gently lifting Gary into a sitting position. He wheezed and his eyes, white with pain, rolled back.

The doctor glanced around for a nurse and swore. "There's no time. Help me hold this." He cocked his arm and stabbed the syringe into Gary's back. With my arms around my husband, I watched a thick blackish-brown fluid fill the syringe. The doctor met my eyes and explained shortly, "You were right. His lungs were filled with fluid." He eyed the tubing that hung from the bucket, anger darkening his expression. "You see this? The night nurse must have set up this bucket and tube system so she wouldn't have to feed your husband ice chips. He was drowning."

Needless to say, the nurse lost her job.

When we weren't in hospitals, the days at home could be just as hard. Gary was a proud man, used to being in control, and having a disease that renders you helpless didn't suit him well. He would shout at me, bellow for me to leave him. "I don't love you anymore," he swore, "I want you gone."

As much as his hurtful words stung, I forced him to talk to me. "Gary, this isn't you. This is the disease. Come back to me, Gary."

"I don't want to talk." His face shut off, and he'd turn away, closing in on himself in his wheelchair.

"We can get through this," I wheedled, trying to grab his hand. He jerked it away. "Let's pray about it. Come on, Gary!"

"Just leave me alone!" Wheeling around, he started down the hall. After a moment, I always walked after him, to try and calm him down. Gary began to pray about more things. I was amazed at the changes in him.

But he still could get discouraged. It got even worse after he was diagnosed with an aneurysm in 2003 that extended from the aorta in his heart.

In 2011, surgeons decided it was too risky to operate, and Gary lashed out. He felt he was given another death sentence.

"You don't get it, Sherrie!" he shouted one fall day. "You don't know what it's like to be trapped in a body like this!"

"Gary, I just want you to talk to me! I just wish you weren't so angry all the time!"

"And why shouldn't I be angry?" he roared, gripping the rubber of his wheelchair armrests. "Every year, it's something else."

I burst into tears, covering my face. "Gary, God's always been so faithful to us."

"Why isn't God answering our prayers now?" Sarcasm dripped thick as hate off Gary's tongue. "Why don't you get it, Sherrie? I'm always under attack."

"Is this where you tell me to leave again?" I couldn't keep the bitterness out of my voice.

"Why not? You know you want to! My hands don't

work, I can't always feed myself, my speech is slurred and I lose consciousness every month. It's too hard for you."

"I made a promise to God! Forever and always! That may not mean anything to you, but it means something to me!" I spun and loped toward our room, wiping away the hot tears streaming down my cheeks. After a year of trying to talk, all I had left was silent exhaustion.

"Aw, honey."

I started past the kitchen down the hall.

"Sherrie, I'm sorry." Wheels rolled over the carpet. "Sherrie, come on."

"Go away."

The small shrill note of an electronic engine using all its power pinged in the air as the wheelchair raced after me. "Sherrie, come on! Talk to me! We can pray about it."

I whirled around and burst out laughing. The sight of my husband chasing after me in his wheelchair after spending most of his life running from communication was too funny for me to stay mad. Gary looked down and chuckled. Then he held out his hand. I knelt beside him, and we both bowed our heads. "Dear God …"

We learned to forgive. Over and over.

As time went on, Gary became a different man. A man who was kind, thoughtful and gentle. A man who prayed about everything. Never mind that he was in a wheelchair. I called him my prayer warrior.

༈ ༈ ༈

FOREVER AND ALWAYS

I know it sounds like a miserable life, in and out of hospitals, but we've honestly been quite happy. Sherrie's never-wavering love for God, her devotion to our sons and I and her optimistic faith kept us going through the hard times. Since I wasn't a workaholic like I was when my oldest son, Craig, was small, I was given a second chance to spend more quality time with all three sons, even if I do regret they spent much of their childhood wondering if I'd make it to their next birthday. Though our life was chaotic, we were able to give them a stable, loving home, watching their sports games and attending church and school events. Each of them grew to become Godly men — men of nobility, integrity and love for their families.

Prayer became an increasingly important part of my life. For a man who had always been in charge of my own destiny, it was humbling to admit I didn't have all the answers and to put my confidence in God. But I truly believe that until I surrendered, most of my medical ordeals were lessons. Apparently, I needed to repeat the lesson several times to finally get it. My self-sufficiency finally turned to surrender.

Now it was time to learn to help others. After years of caring for her mother full time in our home, and then me, Sherrie faced some health challenges. She was diagnosed with fibromyalgia and a crushed disc that gave her pain in her hips, legs and back. "I'm just so tired," she said wearily, curled up on her bed. Years of sleeping only four hours a night and caring for an entire family had taken their toll, and menopause had delivered the final blow. We hired a caregiver to come to the house two hours a day to do the heavy lifting, which put us on equal footing for the first time in years. She was no longer the full-time caregiver, and I was no longer her patient. We were husband and wife again, excited to go on dates and reclaim part of our marriage that had been stolen.

But the one thing we've always been able to do well is celebrate. We've enjoyed some great family trips to places like the Grand Canyon, Canada, Hawaii, plus cruises. One of the best decisions was to see a marriage counselor, who is helping both of us create a kinder marriage. I realized I didn't have to be afraid of counseling — I just had to be willing to change and take responsibility for my actions. I used to run our marriage like I ran my business. After 36 years, it's amazing how we only get deeper in love. Only God could do that.

One night, while our sons bustled around with their families helping fix dinner for a family cookout, Sherrie sat next to me and took my hand. "Did you ever imagine when you met me at the car dealership this is what our life would be like?"

I kissed her hand. "I didn't, but I always hoped."

"I'm sure you thought you'd be like Donald Trump," she teased, smoothing back my hair.

"You got it all wrong," I told her. "I'm much richer than he'll ever be. Look how much God did for us — and it's worth it all." I winked. "He let me marry an angel. After all, you and God are indispensible."

She smiled. "Forever and always."

FOREVER AND ALWAYS

"Till death do us part," I agreed.

Hand in hand, she walked and I rolled to join our family for dinner.

LOOKING FOR LOVE IN ALL THE WRONG PLACES
The Story of Ingeborg Weybright
Written by Miranda Koerner

"Dad, it's really late." My teenage sister Marie yawned, shifting in the front seat. "We need to get Ingeborg and the little ones home."

"Just a few more blocks." My dad hunched over the wheel, his knuckles white from twisting and turning down lanes only *her* memory haunted. He scanned the empty streets, desperation carved in every wrinkle of his forehead.

"Dad, she's not here." Marie shook his arm, but he only turned down another road. "Dad, she's gone."

"No, she's not." His voice was low, but my young ears picked up the need, the panicked urgency. "She's not gone. She can't be. She wouldn't leave you kids. She'd never leave you kids."

"Dad, she's probably —" My sister glanced back, and I shut my eyes, closing them just long enough for her to inspect my face and turn back. "She's probably with *him* again."

He slammed on the brakes. I pelted forward but kept my eyes shut. His breathing remained slow and controlled.

"She's just lost. She's sick. She's not in her right frame of mind."

TOTAL RESTORATION

But his logical reasons were delivered with a plea we couldn't pretend we didn't hear. Even when she came back a few days later, smelling of a strange aftershave, she had left a long time ago. All that was left was a shell of a woman hollowed out by illness, staring at my infant brother and the rest of us like strangers she used to know in a house she used to visit. My father never said a word, going to work and coming home like it was the most normal thing in the world to have a dying wife who would have walked out at any moment. Until he buried her, he clung to the hope she would come back, that everything would be all right. A staunch Danish man in body and soul, his love for her was his only weakness. Loving a person that caused him agony and heartache trapped him.

Too bad history repeats itself.

❧❧❧

A girl is supposed to have her mother. She's not supposed to have an older sister serving as a surrogate parent to both her siblings and her grieving father, or a cold grandmother that served glares instead of chocolate chip cookies. When you lose a parent at a young age, you never quite fill the hole because you don't know how. It's easy for adults to rationalize why a person is gone or say they're in a better place, like all the black-clad strangers did at my mother's funeral.

In the casket, she lay still and pale, her arms crossed over her waist. I glanced up at my uncle, dabbing away tears with a white handkerchief like all the other adults. "Is she sleeping?"

His voice sounded thick. His rough fingers smoothed over my hair, and he coughed. "No, she's not sleeping, child."

All I could do was crane my head up to my sobbing uncle and whisper, "Are you sure?"

To this day, I still don't remember much of my mother. I don't remember her face or her laugh or the scent of her perfume. Her long dark hair and dark Native American eyes mirrored mine, but my short blocky stature was all my dad's.

When the flowers had all crumpled and the casserole dishes were empty, my tears flowed under the hot blasts of the shower. Even at 8 years old, I knew nothing would ever be the same again.

One afternoon, I was wiping my nose on the shower curtain when my sister busted in. "Marie!" I ducked behind the thin plastic, blushing. "You have to knock!" I informed her. I was 8 now. A lady, not a child needing help in the bath.

"You have to stop." She crossed her arms and stared at me, ignoring my squirming to cover myself.

"Stop what?" I hissed.

"Stop crying. The whole house can hear you. She's gone. Nothing can change that." Handing me a towel, she left as abruptly as she had come. I climbed out of the bath and stared at my red-rimmed eyes and swollen nose. Tears welled up, and I dabbed them away, the soft cloth rough against the pink edges. They would be the last tears I shed over my mother for a long time.

But I wanted to cry. It wasn't enough that my father walked around like a zombie and my sister doled out chores and orders like a miniature domestic Napoleon. At school, my friends skirted around me like I was a rabid beast.

"Your mother is dead," one pointed out, wrinkling her nose.

"What's it like?" a curious little girl asked.

I shrugged. "She's dead."

"That's so weird," another girl said, shuddering.

"Weird," they agreed.

After my mother's death, we moved into a small apartment connected to my grandmother's house. My grandmother had barely tolerated my own mother, let alone grandchildren she wanted nothing to do with. Her husband, my step-grandfather, was thrilled to have us. Or, at the very least, thrilled to have me. A grizzly of a man with permanent red cheeks and a broad nose with nostrils that flared like a bull's, he paid special attention to my sister and me. Attention neither one of us wanted.

"You think you're so slick," he'd snarl to my sister when she headed for a walk on the beach. "Probably going to meet a boy. You want to show your sister what a slut you are?"

I froze, but my sister just shook her head. "I'll be back in a couple hours." She gave me a brief smile before slipping out, leaving me with a house full of relatives I barely knew and a grandmother that hated us all. One day, in the middle of the living room while my cousins played and my aunts and uncles chatted around us, my step-grandfather pulled me onto his lap. He pulled a blanket over us, forcing my knees up so the fabric sagged between them. With one hand firmly fixed around my waist, he slid his hands up my skirt.

"Now you're going to be a good girl and not scream," he muttered into my ear, his eyes on the rest of the room. I shut my eyes and whimpered.

"Good girl. Good girl." Every breath reeked of a bar, tinged with booze and cigarettes. Finally, he slid me off his lap, pulling the blanket off. I jumped up and ran to my room, crawling into my closet and shutting the door. I was never coming out again. And I would have stayed if my sister hadn't insisted I come eat dinner. I took one look at her exhausted face and bit my lip. How could I tell her? She would be so angry with me. And who knew what my grandmother would say? Instead, I kept quiet.

Since we were basically living with my grandmother, the relatives felt they had the right to say or do whatever they wanted about our situation. They flocked around my dad, offering advice. "You should stay with Sally. Mom's got a place up north."

When he didn't respond to their real estate offers, the bidding war began. "I'll take Marie."

"Ingeborg and her brother can stay with me," my mother's sister offered, trying to hide her gleeful smile.

I glanced at my dad, then back at my sister. "I don't want to go with them! I want to stay with you!"

"Your father has to work, child," my grandmother growled. "He can't expect to take care of four kids on his own." She shook her head. "I've raised my children, but I could take one." She eyed my sister hopefully. I clutched onto her arm. My grandmother wasn't exactly the cookie-baking type. She was more the type to bake children into cookies.

"No one is going anywhere." My father raised his head. His bloodshot eyes blazed with grief. "You don't break up a family. There's work in Reedsport, at the cheese factory. We'll move there."

My grandmother pursed her lips. "Suit yourself. But don't come crawling to me when you have problems wrangling all these kids."

This time, my sister answered. "We won't."

As I was to learn, men lied.

We were separated that summer, but at least it was only for a summer. We bounced between two aunts, who were as different as day and night. One aunt was sweet and funny with open arms and constant giggles that flowed like water. Our other aunt was cold and stern, and her husband wasn't much better. Bounding down the stairs one day, I heard the angry current of voices mumbling. I crept around the corner and waited, peeking around the doorframe.

"When are these darn kids leaving?" My uncle crunched his bacon hard, his knife slicing through his pancakes like a surgeon through flesh. "I nearly killed myself on Dylan's tennis shoes. And the grocery bill is going to eat me alive."

"It's only another week," my aunt sighed, barely looking up from the paper. "You can deal with it until then."

I stumbled back, hurt and pain radiating from my heart to my toes. My mother didn't want me. My father couldn't take care of me. Not even my aunts or uncles wanted me. Not caring if they heard me, I stumbled out the back door and hit the streets, desperate to find someone with a kind smile and friendly words.

❧❧❧

I knew my father loved me, but he wasn't verbal about it. "Dad, I love you," I'd say.

He'd say nothing. "Dad, I love you," I'd say for weeks and months.

One day, he said, "That's nice."

Encouraged, I kept saying it, every day. "Dad, I love you." He never replied.

Another day, he'd say, "I feel the same way."

Finally, years later, he said, "I love you, too." It thrilled me. Finally I heard the words I longed to hear.

In high school, I determined to seek out the love and attention I never found in my childhood. I did all the right things and made all the right friends with all the right people to accomplish my goal. A cheerleader dating an athlete, my life appeared perfect. Underneath, my carefully constructed charade of happiness threatened to crack. My friends just liked me because of my status, and most boys liked me because I batted my eyes, tossed my hair and made them feel like they were the kings of everything.

When I met Miles, everything changed. I stood on the beach in Oregon watching a long, lean surfer hit the waves. Barefoot and in shorts, he paddled out. Instantly, I knew I was gone. I didn't care that his hair was thinning or that he was four years older — I was smitten. By fall, I was pregnant with his child.

After searching for love for so long, after I found it, I wasn't quite sure what to do with it. So I threw it away. I called Miles. "I'm breaking up with you."

"What?" His normally easy tone rose in surprise. "What's wrong?"

"Nothing's wrong. I just —" I swallowed back tears and rested a hand on my belly. "I don't feel the same way."

"But, Ingeborg —"

"Oh, forget it. Just go to Hawaii and surf. I know you don't want to be here, anyway."

"What?" Suspicion clouded the receiver. "Are you pregnant?"

"No! Why would you ask me that?" I lied.

"Ingeborg, if you're pregnant, then we can get married. I'll be here for you and the baby."

"I'm not pregnant, I'm breaking up with you! What part of this don't you understand?" I slammed down the phone and burst into tears.

Much to my dismay, I was a great actress. Miles packed up and moved to Hawaii, leaving me with a disappointed father.

"I don't understand you, Ingeborg," he sighed a month later. The thick agony of his voice washed over me like a monsoon. "You're not married!"

"I'm sorry."

I stared at the floor at the spaces between my toes. My toenail polish was chipped.

"And Miles! His parents run this town, are highly regarded and very proper!"

"I'm sorry." No matter how many times I said it, it would never be enough. The look on my dad's face was pure sorrow. It was the look of a man whose heart had been broken too many times. But his next whisper brought me to tears.

"So am I, Ingeborg."

The next day, I called Miles in Hawaii. "Hi."

"Hi."

"I lied."

He was quiet a moment. "You're pregnant?"

"Yup."

"Are you sure?"

I sighed. "Of course I'm sure!"

"Well, considering you just told me a month ago you weren't, I don't know about that," he retorted.

"I am sure! I just lied."

"Well, that's mature," he drawled, sarcasm edging his voice. "When are you going to grow up?"

"Oh, really? This coming from a man who surfs all day?"

"I'm coming out there. We're getting married."

I clasped onto the phone. The snarky reply dried on my lips. "Really?"

"Really. See you in a few days."

I sighed. Things were going to be okay.

"Hey, Ingeborg?"

"Yeah?"

"I love you."

The three words I always wanted to hear were finally falling from a pair of lips that meant them. "I love you, too."

True to his word, Miles came home. A few days after he came home and told his parents our news, I received a letter in the mail. The second I looked at the return address, my stomach dropped.

"Who's that from?" My dad nodded to the envelope as I tore it open, taking out the folded paper with shaking fingers.

"It's from Mile's mom," I said, unfolding it and scanning the delicate handwriting.

"What'd she say?" My dad peered over my shoulder, reading the delicately written words along with me.

Dear Ingeborg, I know this isn't the plan you had for your life. This isn't the plan Miles had for his. But things happen for a reason. Just know we will stand by you and support you. We are thrilled to have you and the baby in our life.

LOOKING FOR LOVE IN ALL THE WRONG PLACES

For the first time, hope bloomed in my chest. I looked at my dad. He coughed and turned his head so I couldn't see his smile. "You better invite them over for dinner. What a nice lady."

With both families standing behind us, we got married and had our son, then a second son a few years later. We traded late-night dates for diapers, and Miles traded surfing for a 9 to 5. Trapped with two small children in the house, I craved a release.

By 1975, only a few years after we exchanged vows, our marriage had turned from husband and wife to roommates sharing babysitting duties. When Miles wasn't working, he played baseball, surfed, hunted or hung out with his friends, while I was stuck at home with two kids in the country without any socialization or outlet. I longed to go back to school or find a job, anything to make me feel like there was more to life than picking up toys and changing diapers.

"I want a divorce," I told Miles one day, chopping vegetables for dinner.

"No, you don't." He pulled the fridge open and grabbed a soda. "You're just frustrated."

"I do want a divorce. You're never home, anyway."

He cracked the top and took a swig. "I work 50 hours a week. I'm allowed to have fun."

I slammed the knife into the cutting board. "I don't love you anymore."

He stood, the can halfway to his lips. I didn't need to say the words again. He set the can down carefully and walked to the garage. Putting his hand on the doorknob handle, he paused. What he said next was only a whisper, but I heard it loud and clear. "Lord, if you heal my marriage, I'll follow you to the ends of the earth." Then he slammed the door behind him, and I heard the engine of his car roaring as the garage door pulled up. Our son ran into the room, and I wiped my eyes on my shirt.

He glanced at the door, then at me. "Why are you crying, Mommy?" His lip trembled. "Where's Daddy going?"

"Daddy had to go to work, baby." I wiped my eyes and kept chopping.

"Why are you crying?"

"Just the onions," I said, sniffling. He eyed me and nodded, returning to his game. I resumed chopping carrots for dinner.

There wasn't a single onion on my board.

A few weeks later, some friends told us about Hauser Hills Community Church, and we decided to go, mostly because neither one of us knew what to do about our marriage. Slowly, over time, I began to soak in the teachings of the church and fall back in love with my husband. Though Miles was raised in a Christian family and had roots in church, my own father was a good man, but not a church-going one. As I learned about the Gospel and all the stories in the Bible, a feeling of peace infused me. At the same time, I began learning about my husband all over again through church studies and groups held in people's homes. The man whose children I had born changed from the man I met on the beach that one day. I was changing, too, becoming the woman I had always wanted to be. One day during a church service, I reached over and took Miles' fingers, entwining them with my own. I stared at our two rings, side by side, hand in hand. For the first time, I really felt married.

Shortly thereafter, we moved. Miles took on a new job, we signed the boys up for school and sports and I got involved at our new church. Life was good. We grew in our marriage, and our children grew and settled in at college.

One day Miles looked at me.

"Did you hear about that mission project in the Philippines?"

I nodded.

"I think we should go."

I nearly fell out of my chair. "What?"

"I feel like we need to go. I feel like I'm being called."

I glanced around at our house, at the cozy furniture and memories all over the walls. "It's expensive, isn't it?"

"We can raise money." He pointed to our television. "We can sell some things, and I can work overtime."

"The Philippines?" I let out my breath slowly. "Are you sure?"

He pressed his lips together, his green eyes serious. "I made a promise, Ingeborg."

If you heal my marriage, Lord, I will follow you to the ends of the earth.

If I had learned one thing over the past 20 years with

this man, it was that we were better together than apart. "I'm coming with you."

His smile lit up my heart. "Really?"

"Really."

It wasn't until after we sold everything we owned and actually moved there that I regretted ever agreeing to come. By then, I wasn't quite sure God wanted me there, either.

ॐॐॐ

After I had my second son, due to some health issues, I had to have a hysterectomy. Since I couldn't stomach the hormone replacement pills they gave me, I wore a patch. In the Philippines' hot, sticky weather, the patch was as useless as a band-aid in the swimming pool. Weight began to fall off me. I was so nauseous I couldn't eat, and hot flashes in tropical weather made me as miserable as a polar bear in July.

The worst part was, I couldn't go home. We had sold our home and everything we owned just to come to the Philippines. Even if I left, there was nowhere to go home to. I felt trapped in a foreign land without the medicine I needed, emotionally and physically exhausted.

One day, I stood under the running shower, weeping. "Dear Lord, please heal me. Please tell me what to do." My tears mixed with the water, trailing down my cheeks. "I'm so sick. Please, please let me go home."

Over my sobs, I heard the strains of "Be Still My Soul,"

a hymn from church. It was a high clear voice no radio or human could have produced. I felt certain it must be an angel, singing just for me. Suddenly, the same feeling of peace I'd had when I first came to church washed over me, and my tears stopped. I stood in the shower, soaking up the joy like a dried sponge left in the sun for too long. When I got out and toweled off, I heard voices downstairs. A family had come to visit us, and their teenage son eyed our piano.

"Do you play?" I asked.

He nodded shyly.

"Can you play 'Be Still My Soul'?"

He nodded again and raced to the keys. The second his fingers hit the keys, the song poured over me like angels themselves were singing. It was a peace that Miles, as much as I loved him, could have never brought me. The warm content humming in my heart was the gentle lullaby of the sweet words of Jesus himself. This time, I was going to listen.

I left the Philippines soon after that, and Miles followed a few weeks later. Even though he never said anything, I felt terribly guilty. Going to the Philippines was his dream, and I had dragged him back to no house, a bad economy and few job prospects. We both did anything we could to put food on the table. Miles dug ditches, and I cleaned houses. Finally, he got a job at the paper mill, and we managed to buy a little house before the mill went out of business. Miles began to take classes to be a real estate appraiser.

One day, deep in depression over my illness, I saw the old black veil of sorrow and ugliness move in front of my face.

"I know you," I whispered, staring at its shadow reflected in the television. "I know you, and I'm not going to let you take me."

I stood up, facing myself in the mirror. "I'm not going to be miserable anymore," I growled, ripping the shadows clinging to my face and eyes. "I'm not going to writhe in self-pity. I'm strong. We'll get through this."

"Ingeborg?" I turned around. Miles stared at me from the doorway. "Are you okay?"

I smiled. Walking over to him, I twined my arms around his neck. "I love you."

"I love you, too." He kissed me. "You know we're going to be okay, right?"

"I know." I kissed him back. "As long as we're together, we always will be."

He smiled. Not a single shadow drifted over his face or mine. There was a shield around us, soft as angels' wings but strong as steel. We had God, and we had each other. That was all we needed, and no evil thoughts or deeds could come between us again.

Since then, as long as we've been together and remain strong in our faith, things have been all right. As long as we stay confident in the Lord, he leads us down the right path, no matter what problems come our way. We've had health problems, battles with identity theft and ups and downs in the job market; but we've also experienced enormous joy with the births of our granddaughters and our relationships with wonderful family and friends. We have a new family at Living Faith Assembly of God that helps us grow closer as a couple and makes us better as people every day.

Sitting on our back porch watching the sunset, I turn to Miles as he comes in from fishing on the lake, water beading on his shoes. "Good fishing?"

"Oh, yeah." He sits down next to me. Even now, with the white and grey peppering his beard and the crinkles etched around his wise green eyes, I still see a ghost of the boy I saw on the beach years ago. He wraps his hand around mine. "I love you."

I smile. Those words echo deep within me, from a voice not his, but from above.

For it took a long time, but I finally found a love that would love me back.

CLEAR SKIES
The Story of Janet
Written by Arlene Showalter

"What are you doing?" Mother screamed. She ripped me out of my bed and grabbed the nearest weapon she could get her hands on — a slender stick on which a balloon bobbled. I'd received it at a parade a few hours earlier. Now, she used it to whip me.

Afterward, she dressed me in long sleeves and pants, in the middle of summer, until all evidence of her rage faded. What was my offense? Playing in my crib when I'd been told to take a nap.

I was 2. I never forgot that beating.

ॐ ॐ ॐ

Mother birthed three children in as many years. I was sandwiched between my smarter, older sister and apple-of-her-eye, younger brother. Mother doted on Shawn, screamed at Jean and unleashed her wrath on me. I had no idea at the time that she'd grown up with an abusive mother — and she didn't know how to do things differently. Having three children close together must have made her feel overwhelmed and inadequate. Those feelings were vented on us.

Dad fell in love with the Flathead Lake Valley in Montana and moved us there before I was 5. As the largest freshwater lake west of the Mississippi River, it offers 160 miles of shoreline and plenty of aquatic fun. We three built rafts, swam in the lake, played army, dug ditches and built forts. We lived in paradise. Many families came to the lake for summer vacations, and we played with their children. But as soon as fall arrived, the other kids evaporated to their homes and schools, and we were left to entertain ourselves.

Shawn enjoyed his status as perfect child and baby of the family, until Jo came along 10 years later. By that time, the family dynamic was set in concrete.

৵৵৵

My second grade teacher mirrored my mother with vengeful rantings. Each morning I left a home of simmering anger to face a teacher with her own furious agenda. One day she grabbed me by my dress, popping all the buttons in front, before heaving me toward her desk, where I spent the majority of my school year huddled under it, along with Donald, the only other redhead in the class.

She hates redheads, I thought. *Mother must hate redheads, too. I'm the only one in all our family with red hair and freckles. I'm the only left-handed one.* As I sat under Mrs. Crabapple's desk, I mulled over my life to date. *Why am I so different? I must be adopted. That's why she hates me so much. I don't belong. I have no value.*

Anger against Mother and Mrs. Crabapple built up

inside me. I longed to fight back, but the consequences of taking on the bigger and angrier women frightened me. I scrambled to find release, but where? How? When I thought I'd explode, I grabbed clumps of hair and yanked them out, from my head, my arms, my eyelashes.

"The craziest thing happened," Mother would say, "just after Shawn was born. I found you in your crib with every single strand of hair yanked out and lying on the mattress. Whatever would make an 18 month old do that?"

I sure didn't know and never pulled it all out again. Just a bit here and a bit there, enough to release my own rage and get on with the misery of life.

అలలల

Seventh grade brought on a new angst. I developed dermatitis on my arms and face. The sores itched and oozed and grew worse the following year. I wore a ton of makeup to cover it. Self-confidence dribbled from naught to nothing.

"You have your speech ready?" my teacher asked.

"Won't do it," I said.

"You'll get an F."

I shrugged. "I'd rather take the F. I'm not getting up in front of anybody."

I found a way to anesthetize myself against my self-loathing and feelings of worthlessness. Both my parents smoked, and Dad rolled his own cigarettes. Stealing from his stash gave me a rush. Smoking them in secret added to the enjoyment.

Then the stoners in school introduced me to marijuana. Tortured thoughts vanished in its fragrant vapor. *I'm cool. I'm wanted. I have value.*

৵৵৵

I discovered one other thing to affirm my otherwise pathetic existence. I learned I could run and fast. I joined the high school track team, running the short distances. My feet exploded from the blocks as I could not allow the anger fermenting within me to do. The ability to sprint put me on the fastest relay team in the state, and we held that title for more than six years.

Dad came to some of my meets. At those times, he'd discuss my performance and stats with my coach, all the while resting his hand on my neck. I savored the attention, feeling I was in heaven with his approval.

Mother saved all her energy for Shawn's activities.

I lived dual lives: hanging out with the stoners to forget the crap at home and then around the jocks, who were focused on keeping their bodies clean and healthy to improve their running times.

৵৵৵

"Hey, Janet, how ya doing?" The tall stranger smiled down at me as I waited for my next race. "I'm Dave."

"Hi," I said. "What do you run?"

"The 440 and relay."

"I run relay, too."

"I know." He smiled again. "Fastest in the state. Good for you."

"Thanks," I said. *Be nice if my own mother acknowledged it. She'd be shouting from the housetops if it were Shawn.*

We spent many hours together at the track meets, discussing sports.

"How would you like to work out with me?" he asked. Elation filled me. *He likes me. He likes me for me.*

"That'll be cool."

"Want to study together?" he asked later on.

"Sure," I said. He gave me his address, a farm some 45 minutes from my house. I pedaled my bike there often, the minutes flying as I delighted in my new friendship. *He still likes me, even though he's smart and I'm not. And he's such a great kid and funny.*

My confidence grew with our friendship. I had value. I had purpose. The hair pulling all but stopped.

Dad and Mom ran a small art gallery in town. We kids worked there when Dad was busy showing properties as a real estate agent.

"I'll pick you up at the gallery this afternoon," Dave told me on a summer day just before our senior year of high school.

"Great," I said. As closing time approached, I checked the clock over and over again. Although we'd not taken the step from friendship to relationship, Dave and I enjoyed the many hours we spent together. Amazement still filled me that such a sweet, kind, good-looking hunk cared for me at all.

The appointed time came. I hurried to close the store. No Dave.

I scrutinized every car that approached. None looked familiar. A sick feeling settled in my stomach. I hopped on my bike, riding to every likely and not-so-likely place in search of him.

"Have you seen Dave?"

"No."

A deepening sense of dread piled up along with each no I heard. Nobody knew Dave's whereabouts.

I took myself home, hope draining from me like a slow leak in an inner tube.

"I can't find Dave," I told Dad.

"We'll go look around the lake," he said. He left with Mom and our neighbors. *Something's wrong, I just know it.* I sat on the front lawn, my stomach roiling with anxiety. *He's always been so reliable. He'd never stand me up. He always keeps his word. Always.*

Other neighbors drove by. "Hey, we heard some kid drowned in the lake," the man shouted.

"Do you know who?" I asked.

"Didn't recognize the name," he said. "Sorta like Triplet."

Close enough to Dave's last name, Tripp. *It's him. He's gone.*

A rescue team recovered his body the next day. Dave

had been riding on the back of a Skidoo with a friend when the wake of a passing boat flipped the machine. He hadn't worn a life vest. The boy who knew how to make an unwanted, unloved redhead feel special couldn't swim.

Jean and I had business in town that next day and just happened to pull up on the highway directly behind the hearse bearing Dave's body — my sole reason for existence.

"I'm so sorry, Janet." Jean squeezed my hand.

I felt nothing.

ॐॐॐ

Shortly after I lost Dave, my sister moved 300 miles away for her first year of college. Overwhelmed with his death, Mother's rages and my own inadequacies, I ran. *To her.* I hit the highway, hitchhiking east.

"Hop in," one driver said. "Where you headed?"

Something about him brought back that familiar dread in my stomach. I named the next city.

"Too bad," he said. "It would be fun to travel together."

My mind raced. "Oh," I said, forcing nonchalance, "sorry. My aunt is expecting me, and I'm already late."

"I could show you a good time."

"Yeah." I shrugged. "But you know how grownups are. If I don't show up, she'll have every cop in the state out."

"Yeah," he agreed. "You're right."

I guided him down a few streets, my mind keeping just

ahead of his wheels. "Turn right here. She's the third house on the right."

He stopped at the house I pointed out.

"I'll wait till you get inside," he offered.

"Oh, please, don't do that. She'll freak out if she knows I hitchhiked. Goodbye, and thanks for the ride."

I strode into the backyard and hid until I heard him drive away. Then I waited a few minutes longer to make sure he didn't return, hoping he didn't see through my ruse. I crept out of the strange yard to a nearby college and bedded down in their dorm.

I returned to the highway the next morning, still shaken. Another kid stood by the road with his thumb hanging out.

"Hey, lady." The pleasant-faced boy smiled wide. "You going east?"

"Yes, I am," I said.

"How far?"

I named my sister's city.

"Cool," he said. "I'm going there, too. Want to go together?"

My whole being relaxed. For some unknown reason, I felt so safe with him. *Is he a guardian angel?* We hitched a ride, chatted like old friends and parted at our mutual destination.

"Be safe," he said.

"Thank you." I waved and turned to find Jean.

"What are you doing here?" she asked.

"I don't know." I shrugged.

I just need to be near you right now.

She studied me, a worried expression on her face. "You realize I have to call Dad and tell him you're here."

"I know."

My dad bought a ticket, and I took the bus toward home and my senior year. Depression and anger settled into my being. What I needed was Jean, and she wasn't there. Home was overwhelming. I thought about praying, then reconsidered. *Yeah, right,* I thought. *God's been a big help to me through all Mom's rages and beatings. And he was a really big help the night Dave drowned.*

"I'll show you, God," I raged. "Does it bother you that I've been smoking and drinking? Well, you ain't seen nothing yet."

I stumbled through my last year of school, living in a fog of smoke, booze and drugs. I embraced peyote and hallucinogens. *You won't have to destroy me, God. I'll get the job done without your interference.*

I refused to participate in our high school graduation, choosing to sit in the audience with Dave's older brother, Bill, who'd just finished a stint in the Navy. We shared one strong bond: our love for Dave.

એન એન એન

"Want to come to San Diego with me?" Bill asked just before graduation. "I was stationed there. It's a great place."

"Sure," I said. *I want out of here ASAP.*

"Don't do it," Jean said.

"Don't go," Dad begged. "I'll pay for you to go to college. I don't care if you get Ds and Fs. Just don't go."

I went, anyway.

We rented a tiny cottage steps away from Mission Beach. Drugs flowed in 1971, as vast as the Pacific Ocean. "From now on, I'm Jan," I announced the moment we arrived. I wanted a new life and a new identity and sealed my decision with a legal name change.

"Hi, I'm Jan," I told every new friend, acquaintance, supplier and employer. I got a job at a nearby motel and hit the drug scene harder than the crashing waves.

"I'm going home for a visit," our friend Charles told me a year after my move to California. "Want to come?"

"Where's that?" I asked.

"Near Frisco," he said.

"Sure." Bill was a good guy and treated me right, but he wasn't Dave. I used Bill as a one-way ticket from home, but I wanted Dave. I left everything behind in Southern California, including Bill, and took off north with Charles.

He introduced me to his party-hard friend Al almost as soon as we arrived. He was a big guy with a bigger attitude. Al drank hard, inhaled drugs and had his own grudge against God. We became the perfect match made in hell.

As soon as his preacher dad and family learned I carried his child, they pressured me to "accept Jesus." I complied. *I'll say anything, do anything, to get you people off my back.*

Their second stipulation was Al and I had to marry, ASAP, if not sooner. "We will not have an illegitimate grandchild in the family."

We fulfilled that requirement in his parents' backyard. I wore a borrowed wedding dress, complete with a stained front, flowers snatched from the yard and felt as hideous as I looked. (I informed my own family just before the ceremony, ensuring they'd not have time to come from Montana to California.) *Let's just get this over and done with.*

The only bright spot in this day-from-the-abyss was the beautiful, dainty ring Al's family supplied, which had been in the family for generations.

I held my hand out, admiring it after the brief, unpleasant ceremony, when Al walked up.

"You ever take that ring off," he snarled, "and I'll bite it in half."

I whipped it off in a blink.

He grabbed it and, just as fast, the ring lay in two pieces.

Maybe, just maybe, I've made a mistake here.

❧❧❧

Al had his own issues with feeling valued. Being dyslexic, undiagnosed in those days, he was the butt of family jokes.

"We named him Al so he can spell his own name," they joked.

He took his angry frustration and humiliation out on the mother of his unborn child. Careful not to inflict physical damage while I sheltered his kid in my body, he began belittling me.

"You're so ugly," he said, gazing with contempt as I readied for bed. "Especially when you're naked. Gross."

I endured the daily onslaught of his abuse because it fed into my own beliefs of non-value and aided in my promise to make God sorry for ever tangling with me.

After Edward's birth, Al graduated to contact sports, using my head as his preferred target.

"Where's Al?" his latest boss asked on the phone. Al worked for area dairy farmers, and for some quirky reason, cows demanded to be milked twice a day, on time, seven days a week.

"Don't know."

"He's fired."

Al drifted from job to job, and we followed, moving from house to house.

ले॰ले॰ले॰

"Want to come over tonight?" Charles asked. "Got some good stuff for you to try out."

Always on alert for opportunities to self-destruct, I agreed.

Al and I went over and met heroin. It was love at first shoot-up. It proved to be the one common denominator in our marriage.

We focused on living from fix to fix, high to high, and excelled in our mutual interest.

This is life. This is good. All is at peace in my world. Nothing and nobody can touch me here.

But the moment Al and I began our descent back to reality, the abuse returned. I drifted on heroin-induced euphoric clouds and wallowed in my self-made hell.

I learned I was pregnant again, but I avoided medical attention because my arms screamed my lifestyle. Throughout, I remained rail-thin, gaining only 14 pounds total. I went to a doctor just before my due date.

He came to see me shortly after the baby's birth.

"Are you addicted to heroin?" he asked.

"Oh, no!" I feigned shock. "Of course not."

He looked me over. "Your daughter's heartbeat is irregular."

Wonder of wonders, the hospital released Ann into my care.

I endured Al's relentless beatings, both verbal and physical, lived for the next fix and dreamed of suicide. I slit my wrists. *Ugh. That was painful. Don't think I'll try that again.*

I cast around for other solutions. *If I can just get Al angry enough to shoot me and put me out of this misery.*

I went out of my way to goad him, hoping and longing to trigger enough anger to end it all, which brought on more beatings but no hell-relieving bullets. I maintained my lifelong habit of tearing hair from my head, arms and lashes to relieve a smidgeon of stress.

My plan of revenge against God continued to backfire in my own face.

We moved yet again, this time into an upstairs apartment with suppliers conveniently living below us. One night the police came after Don and Pete. We watched from our windows as they tossed their stash into the front yard. The police cuffed the guys and then searched the area. They failed to locate the cast-off drugs, so they hauled the guys off to jail.

Al and I went down and retrieved the heroin. We sold some and used the rest.

A few days later, a big dude I'd never seen before banged his fist on our door.

"Where's Al?" he demanded.

"I don't know," I said, "he's not here." The guy turned, and I saw the gun stuck in his belt.

I have to get out of here, I thought, *before the kids and I get killed. What can I do? Where can I go?*

I thought of Jean, the only rock I'd known in my life. *I'll call her. If I sense the slightest hesitation, I'll just … I don't know what I'll do, but I'll find something.*

I dialed her number. "Jean, I need to find a place to live and fast."

"You come here," she said.

No hesitation. I breathed the first clear air in years.

"I'm going to visit my sister," I told Al.

"Not with Edward, you're not."

"Just Ann." I kept my voice even, but my heart raced. *I have to get out of here.*

I left everything behind, including my husband and son, as I traveled north.

Even though angry at God and refusing to believe him capable of the slightest show of goodness, a ride from California to Washington materialized like a miracle. Pondering the danger I'd escaped, the moment Ann and I climbed into the car, I made a decision. *I'm done with drugs.* I quit, cold turkey, and suffered no withdrawal.

I got a job and an apartment. People who knew Jean donated everything I needed, from clothes to appliances. I started going to her church. The people there welcomed me with openness.

One day, while listening to a girl singing about God's love, I felt him right where I sat in the service.

He accepts me, I felt deep in my being. *I don't understand it, and I don't know why, but right now I feel so accepted and loved by him. I want to be part of his family.*

I came to save you from yourself. I felt God's whisper, in my heart. The lifelong fog I lived in lifted from my mind and heart, and the all-consuming anger that had propelled me for six years abated.

"I accepted Jesus as my personal Savior," I told Jean on our way home.

Three months after I'd left him, Al arrived at my door with Edward, and he moved into my apartment.

"What else am I supposed to do?" I shrugged when I told Jean. "He's my husband. What other options do I have?"

Al brought his abusive habits with him, adding the children as targets of his verbal assaults. Again, he couldn't keep a job.

Soon I found myself pregnant.

"I can't do this," I told Jean. "I can't have another child with this man."

"What will you do?" she asked.

"I don't want this baby," I said. "Neither does Al. I'm going to abort." I hesitated. "Will you take me to the clinic? You know Al never let me learn to drive."

"I will," she said. "You are my sister. I love you and will stand by you, even though I don't agree with this decision."

"I'm not happy about it, either," I said, "but the alternative of raising another kid with him is worse."

I got the abortion.

Al got a vasectomy.

I got pregnant again almost immediately.

Fists and accusations flew.

Doctors confirmed the vasectomy didn't "take." The fog that had saturated my life returned. *I can't go through that again. I can't ask Jean to participate again by taking me for another abortion.* My heart sank to my toes. *I'll have to go through with this one.*

Right after my second daughter, TJ's, birth, Al's brother offered him a job in Oregon. We moved. Then the brother was suddenly killed.

Another brother offered Al a job back in California. We moved again.

I got a job with a landscaper, which required a driver's license. *Finally, at age 31, I have freedom.*

Then we moved again. Al never gave up drugs and scattered them all over the house like leaves in autumn. Away from my sister, and again away from God, I re-embraced meth. *If you can't lick them, you may as well join them.*

Life spiraled downward again, deeper into that fog of worthlessness and despair.

The local police came knocking at the door just before Ann started her junior year of high school. "We have a warrant to arrest Al," the officer said.

"For what?" I asked.

"Alleged sexual abuse with a minor."

My mind and face went blank.

"What child?"

"Your daughter, Ann."

"You're joking," I said. I turned to her. "How? When?" I scrambled to think. "That's impossible."

"Mom," she screamed, "he's had sexual intercourse with me."

Mind and body numbed. *How can this be?* My thoughts raged in denial, shock. *Under my roof? How could I not know?*

Al left, never to live with me again. He begged Ann to drop the charges, denying everything, but she stood firm.

I went to court with her, mind still reeling. Worthlessness reached a new low. *How could I miss the signs? How could I not protect my own children?*

TOTAL RESTORATION

Drugs helped me ignore the issues but never solved them.

ॐॐॐ

Edward began cultivating marijuana in our backyard. One beautiful, healthy plant to ease us through life's bleakness. Neighbors, ignorant of horticulture, admired our lush plant.

Then one day, I heard TJ screaming her lungs out. I rushed down the hall toward her and never noticed the DEA officer with drawn gun, pointed directly at me.

Edward, who'd been watching from across the street, came home. "That's my plant," he said, indicating the one they'd dug up and bagged for evidence.

They took him, along with Ann, to Juvenile Hall, allowed TJ to stay with a neighbor and arrested me.

After three days, I appeared before the judge. Because of a squeaky-clean record, even after years of hard drugs, he released me.

Next, I went to a hearing at Juvenile Hall and took my kids home.

I filed for and obtained a divorce and changed my name from Jan back to Janet.

A name change certainly didn't help me any, so I may as well go back to my given name.

With my new/old name, I began looking for something different out of life, other than the high drugs offered.

A friend told me about a guy who was trying to start a Western stunt group.

"He's looking for people," he said, "to join his group."

"I'm a people," I said. "It sounds like fun. I'd like to do it."

"Great," he said. "I'll arrange a meeting. His name is Gerald. He used to work with stuntmen at Universal Studios in Hollywood."

Gerald and I worked together a lot, designing and making costumes, working on tricks and writing scripts. I found I enjoyed playing character roles. We worked parades, birthday parties and other events, paid only in tons of fun.

Gerald and I shared more and more of life and, realizing our compatibility, moved in together. When his dad called with a great job opportunity, we jumped on it and moved to Cottage Grove, Oregon.

"My folks want to take us to breakfast tomorrow," Gerald said. *To get us into church afterward, I thought. But I don't mind. They treat me better than Al's parents ever did.*

We enjoyed their church family, and I returned to the relationship I'd begun with Jesus back in my sister's church. Gerald and I became active in the church and put on stunt shows for the children.

Later, we decided to go to another church. After a while, the director there approached me.

"Janet," she said, "you seem very good with children. How would you like to teach a Sunday school class?"

"I'd love to."

She paused. "We have only one small issue," she said. "The church board would prefer that you be married, as an example for the kids."

So, Gerald and I married.

ॐॐॐ

Three months later, I learned my father had terminal cancer. He told us to stay away because he didn't want us to see him in his final days.

"I can't take it," I told Gerald. "I'm going, whether he likes it or not."

Dad lived his life as an atheist. He thought Jesus a great guy but nothing more.

"Dad, you need to understand who Jesus really is and accept him as God and your Savior," Jean and I urged him. "We want to see you again, in heaven. We love you."

Dad got sicker. My conversations with God got more urgent. "You can't take him like this," I prayed.

"I don't want to leave the Flathead Valley," Dad said.

"If you believe in Jesus," I said, "you are going to a better place."

"I don't know." He seemed unconvinced.

I called often, talking to him about Jesus. Jean did the same.

ॐॐॐ

I started a new job at Walmart. After my first day of work, I called my mom the moment I walked in the door. We talked for a few minutes and hung up. An hour later, the phone rang.

"Your dad passed," Mom said.

My heart sank. We still had no verbal assurance from Dad that he'd yielded to God's love. I looked at the clock. *11 p.m. And today is the 11th day of the 11th month.* I kept thinking about those 11s, and suddenly, a deeper peace than I'd ever known in my life settled over me. I felt God's presence more than when I first accepted Jesus as my Savior.

Your dad's okay now, I sensed him say in my spirit. *Do you not understand my love for you, Janet? Do you not know that I'm with you, and I've always been with you?*

I allowed myself to relax fully in God's arms for the first time in my life. I started talking *to* God rather than *at* him. I began returning some of God's love and trust.

ৡৡৡ

After 10 wonderful years in our church, the pastor's son took over the youth department and relegated me to kitchen duty. My anger against God returned with a vengeance.

How can you let this happen to me? I raged. *How can you let "Christians" screw me over like that? It's all your fault, and you're hurting me all over again. My life's just one crappy mess again, and it's all your fault.*

TOTAL RESTORATION

తతత

"I think Good Samaritan Ministries would help you," Jean told me one day in 2005. "They've helped me so much with my own issues from childhood, I became a counselor myself."

"I'm so tired of life as it is. So quick to be angry," I said. "I'll give it a try."

I had somewhat of a good relationship with God, willing to be open and vulnerable to him. However, I never reached out to share or expose myself to humans.

Women came from Good Samaritan's main office in Beaverton and spoke at that first meeting.

"Some people pull their hair out," one explained. "This is self-injurious behavior that manifests itself in a physical act, while hiding the true emotional reason."

Oh, my gosh, I thought, *I've been doing that all my life.* I kept quiet but approached the speaker later.

"I need help," I said. "I've had this behavior all my life."

"How about coming to a session?" she suggested. "We do mock counseling. First, you play the role of counselor, and then later, we switch places."

"I think I can do that," I said, while fear spread its ugliness in my stomach. In the past, I'd often eased my tension by carrying a toy with me. That night, I found a pair of 3-D glasses that my grandson owned, with one red and one green lens, and tucked them into my folder as a security object.

When the role-playing began, I was assigned as counselor. It was fun to be on the asking side of the session. Then the roles switched, and I became the client. Immediately, I felt that familiar discomfort and had to push my chair back. *Too close, way too close.* I fought against a rising panic attack.

I have to get away. What can I do? I remembered the glasses, pulled them from my folder, put them on and grinned.

Everyone laughed but then stopped.

"Do you think this is funny?" the lady in charge asked.

"Yeah," I said.

"Are you hiding?" she asked.

Silence.

"Do you think you are a good person?"

More silence.

"Is there anything good about you?" she asked.

Increasing silence.

"Nothing good about you?"

"No."

I removed the glasses, feeling crappier and crappier by the second, like my entire soul lay exposed in front of all those strangers. Naked. *Nobody would want to see you naked,* Al had mocked. *You're so ugly.*

I waited for the condemnation. The twitters of mocking laughter.

But the silence turned to me, rather than against me.

I feel love.

I feel acceptance.

I'm okay.

"I have an assignment for you," said Gail, the director of GSM. "I want you to write down all the lies you've believed about yourself. Then I want you to write down all the truth you know about yourself."

I did so and stared at the paper. *Amazing.* The truth column ran much longer than the lie side.

I am loved.

I am accepted.

I am loveable.

I am acceptable.

I am good.

I am worthy of love.

I began to understand my mother more. Having never experienced approval from her own mom, she didn't know how to show approval to me. I learned that each of us carries wounds and believes lies about ourselves. Those wounds and lies cause negative behaviors. I still struggle with a tendency to believe the lies that permeated my childhood, but with God's help, I choose to believe what he sees in me.

I joined Good Samaritan Ministries, first as a client, and now, today, I serve as a counselor.

➶➶➶

"Hey, Janet," Gerald said, after he'd returned from a local yard sale. "I met this cool guy today. His name's Randy Fox. We got to talking about guitars, and he told me if I come over to his church, maybe I can play on the worship team."

Church? No, thank you.

"That's nice, if that's what you want to do."

Gerald started going to Living Faith and playing on the worship team. I went to be with him, determined to make little contact and less commitment.

But I worked in landscaping and, after noticing the conditions of the church grounds, couldn't help myself.

"Looking good," the pastor, Rulon, said one day when I was up to my elbows in dirt.

"Thank you."

"Why aren't you playing on the worship team?"

"I will as soon as you get conga drums," I said. I'd never played them in my life.

Living Faith delivered. They got the drums. I played.

Pastor Rulon of Living Faith represented "church authority," something I'd resisted and resented from how Al's parents treated me to the pastor's son who'd casually tossed my 10 years in the youth department aside.

But this pastor's gentleness won me over. He taught me to say yes only when I meant yes and to say no when I wanted to. In my entire life, I always felt an obligation to agree to anything, no matter how much I disagreed with the outcome. Pastor Rulon gave me the freedom to decline and not feel guilty over my decision.

∾∾∾

TOTAL RESTORATION

Even with all the progress, I still had lingering issues as of 2011. Jean suggested I try Cranial Sacral Therapy, a well-researched, specific, non-invasive touch that can support the body's built-in ability to heal. After a few sessions, I was finally able to go to the place where the first wounding began: when I tore every hair from my head at 18 months old.

Mother was busy with her newborn, Shawn. I wanted Mother, but she didn't come. I needed Mother. She didn't come. I was angry with Mother. She didn't come.

How can I hurt Mother? She's not listening to me. She's not meeting my needs. I'm stuck in a crib. What can I do to get her attention? What can I do to make her pay for her inattention to ME?

I tore every strand of hair from my head. And every year that followed, I tore hair from my head and body.

It stopped at that moment of revelation.

ॐ ॐ ॐ

I walked with Jesus when I was 5 years old. We strolled, hand-in-hand, down our country lane after a storm. Rainwater lay in the ruts and holes.

I chattered and chattered, and Jesus listened. When we came to a pothole, I held his hand tighter.

"I don't want your clothes to get dirty." Then I watched his robe swish around the puddle, untainted, and breathed again.

I lifted my nose in the damp spring air and sniffed.

"I love it here, Jesus. I love our lake. And I love you."

I felt his love emanating back to me, through his hand clutching mine. I felt whole.

The fog I lived in all those years swallowed that memory.

God gave it back.

Today I know that lots of crappy things happen and will happen. That's life. But I also know that nothing and no one can affect my value. I am a daughter of God.

I'm good because God created me, and God is good.

I appreciate Pastor Rulon of Living Faith for allowing me to be me. He puts no pressure on me to fit any particular mold, because he knows he is just like me, a human in need of a Savior. He also experiences our Savior's forgiveness and acceptance of us *as is.*

After four decades, I'm paying attention to the lies that affected me for so long. I must be vigilant, since I'm prone to believe a lie before the truth. I built a life around the lies. Though closing my ears to the lies is a battle, God is on my side. And my wounds are healing.

Satan called me worthless. God calls me beloved. Satan called me ugly. God calls me beautiful. Satan says I'm messed up. God says I'm perfect in Christ.

Satan is the ultimate liar. God is ultimate love.

HOPE BEHIND BARS
The Story of Kurt
Written by Karen Koczwara

This is bad. Very, very bad.

My heart thudded in my chest as I followed the police down a flight of stairs. With wide spike-brimmed hats, huge guns and dark slicked-back hair, they were an especially intimidating sight. I felt like a prisoner on death row being led to the electric chair as they marched before me in unison.

I screwed up big time. If they find the drugs, I'm doomed. I don't even want to imagine what they'll do to me. I should have known this was all a stupid idea.

With each dreaded step, my heart thudded faster.

Just keep calm, Kurt. Just play it cool, and maybe you'll get lucky …

మౌమౌమౌ

I was born in 1958 in Long Beach, California, where my father worked in the Navy. A very handsome man, he spent more time pursuing other women than spending time with my mother, my older brother and me. When I was just a year old, my father sat my mother down and announced he didn't love her anymore.

"I am leaving in the morning," he told her.

TOTAL RESTORATION

"No, you are leaving now," she shot back. My mother, quite aware of his skirt-chasing ways, had had enough.

My mother held a job at an aerospace company and had just purchased a brand-new Chrysler with her credit line. My father took off with her car, and away he went. My mother then purchased a blue 1960 VW Beetle as a replacement. She had only recently learned to drive and was a terrible driver. I often hung on for dear life while scrunched in the back compartment.

My mother spent the next few years as a single parent, doing her best to provide for my brother, Pat, and me.

We rented a nice duplex, and a babysitter watched over my brother and me while my mother worked. My grandmother also lived nearby. A wonderful woman, she spoiled us rotten whenever she could. Even when we were old enough to help out around the house, my brother and I were both whiny, selfish slobs who left our bedrooms a complete mess. One day, my mother drove us to the bad part of town and threatened to move us there. As we glanced out at the rundown buildings with peeling paint and sagging fences, we decided it might not hurt to keep our rooms a bit tidier.

Though money was usually tight, my mother always made sure we had whatever we needed. She worked hard and pinched every penny to put clothes on our backs and food in our mouths. Sometimes, she drove us to a trailer nearby, where a woman sat at a sewing machine taking my mother's measurements. I soon learned what our little fieldtrips were all about. My mother, a beautiful woman, could not afford to buy nice dresses, so she had a seamstress make them instead. As a mischievous kid, I was too young to comprehend her daily sacrifices.

One day, I caught my mother crying softly in the bathroom. "Mom, stop faking it," I snapped at her.

But as her bloodshot eyes met mine, I realized she wasn't faking anything. She was genuinely overwhelmed, and my selfish whims weren't helping much.

My mother got a new job at North American Aviation near Los Angeles and began dating her boss in the accounting department. Often, a babysitter watched us while my mother stayed out late. One day, my mother sat my brother and me down with some news.

"Boys, would you like to have a new dad?"

We shrugged. "Yeah, okay." I'd seen the other boys' dads picking them up at school, and yet I seldom saw mine. Having a new dad didn't seem like such a bad thing.

My brother and I waited by the front window for our new dad to arrive one night. When a guy pulled up in a fancy sports car, our eyes grew wide with excitement. *I like him already,* I decided. *He looks pretty cool.*

After their wedding, my mother and Bob whisked us down to San Diego, where we enjoyed a family honeymoon on the beach. Not long after, Bob traded in his sports car for a practical Ford Fairlane station wagon. I was a bit disappointed, as I'd hoped he'd cruise around town with us in his little sports car. But he dove into full-time dad mode, eager to provide a positive influence on two impish little boys.

TOTAL RESTORATION

We moved from Long Beach to Yorba Linda, a new suburb of nearby Orange County. Nestled in the middle of orange groves, the city was in the first stages of development. My brother and I attended the brand-new elementary school there.

In our spare time, we played in the orange groves and climbed the trees. Our new dad bought baseball gloves and tossed the ball around with us after school. We signed up for Little League and the Boy Scouts. Our new grandmother, Bob's mother, was a well-to-do generous, energetic woman we nicknamed "Grandma Babe." She sent us on lavish vacations to Hawaii, and we decided this new family thing was working out pretty well. Long gone were the days of homemade dresses and penny pinching. We were the all-American family now.

My brother took an interest in the guitar, and I grew intrigued with the instrument, too. Two years my senior, my brother was good-looking, smart and popular in school, and I wanted to do whatever he did.

During a weekly shopping trip, I spotted a guitar for $11.77 at Gemco, a local department store. I saved up my money for it and proudly toted it home. My parents bought me music lessons, and I strummed my guitar until my fingers nearly bled. Creedence Clearwater Revival was a popular rock group in the late '60s, and their tunes were easy to play.

My brother moved on to playing the drums, and he and I often jammed together after school. Our music could be heard blocks away from our house, but our parents remained good sports, letting us play to our heart's content.

When I was 11 years old, I joined the contemporary guitar mass at St. Martin's Church on Saturday nights. The group played a mix of contemporary and folk songs, and I was flattered to be a part of it. The mass was my first attempt at any sort of worship music, though I didn't fully understand the words of the songs. As far as I was concerned, the God we sang about was just a nice guy somewhere up in the sky. I became a bit disillusioned when I saw a few of the guys in the choir smoking pot.

I remained active in Boy Scouts and Little League during junior high. On the weekends, we took our mini-bikes out with the neighbors and sped around on them. My brother became interested in dirt bikes and motocross, and I started tagging along with him. We were still a pair of boys who liked to get dirty and have a good time.

In 1973, I started high school at Troy High School in Fullerton. I'd been somewhat sheltered living in the suburbs, and I was initially shocked by the foul language and fighting that took place on my new campus. I quickly learned the ropes at my new school. The "heads" hung out on one end of campus, where they smoked pot and cigarettes. I often heard them talking openly about drugs, and their behavior surprised me. I'd never encountered any kids like this in my clean-cut neighborhood.

My freshman year, I steered clear of trouble. But by my sophomore year, I decided to dabble with cigarettes. When one of my new friends offered me some pot, I didn't turn it down. It was the '70s, after all, the era of flower children, peace, love and rock and roll. I purchased a yellow 1962 Ford van just like my brother's. Complete with a cool eight-track stereo system and plush seats, it also offered lots of room for me to throw my dirt bikes in the back.

I pulled up in the school parking lot with smoke billowing out the windows. The cops often pulled me over for various minor infractions. I knew my van brought unwanted attention and that they found me suspicious. I stuffed away the silly traffic tickets, figuring I'd get around to paying them later.

School was a complete bore and a waste of time for me. Though I was a decent reader, I had no interest in learning. I got a job at a tool supply store in the afternoons and enjoyed bringing home a paycheck. I dated a few girls here and there and continued to skip classes. Not long into my senior year, I decided to drop out of school to work full time. I began working with my brother at a plant nursery, but I quickly got fired for my poor attitude. I then landed a job at a glass shop installing windows and mirrors. I enjoyed it immensely. *Who needs a diploma when you can just get on with life and make money?* I reasoned.

When I was 19 years old, my outstanding traffic tickets finally caught up with me. The cops arrested me for failing to appear in court and threw me in jail for 10 days. I contacted my parents, but they let me sit in there and serve my time. I suspected they hoped I might clean up my act after I got out, but the incident hardly shook me up. I soon returned to my irresponsible ways.

I spent the next few years working at various glass companies and made a decent living. In my early 20s, I discovered cocaine. Famous people were notorious for snorting it, and it seemed cool. I loved the high it offered. I used the drug every chance I got, often spending good chunks of my paycheck on it. Soon, I grew to crave it, and getting more became increasingly important in my life. I grew desperate if I could not get my hands on it and did everything I could to snag some. Before long, my life began to spin out of control.

One day, I walked into the bank where I cashed my paychecks and began chatting with the pretty teller. I noticed her nametag read Marilyn. She told me she was a student at UCLA, and I bragged about my job as well. I'd just gotten a new Ford pickup truck and a promotion at work, which I thought might impress her. We began dating, but it didn't take her long to discover I wasn't as upright as I seemed.

"I know what you're doing, snorting cocaine," Marilyn told me. "I really think you should stop. That stuff is bad news."

I had no interest in stopping, but I also did not want to lose Marilyn. We continued to date off and on for the next several years. She went on to graduate college and then became a successful hotel manager in Orange County. She remained patient with me, encouraging me to escape my destructive lifestyle and get my life back on track. She also invited me to church at Calvary Chapel Costa Mesa, one of the largest churches in Southern California. I enjoyed the music and the casual atmosphere. As the pastor read from the Bible each week, I listened intently. He spoke about a God who loved us so much that he'd sent his son, Jesus, to die on the cross for our sins. He also shared that we could have a relationship with him and spend eternity in heaven with him someday. The message resonated with me. I believed in God and began praying here and there. But I could not kick my drug habit. It consumed me day and night.

I hopped from job to job, somehow always managing to scrounge up enough to pay my bills. But a sizeable chunk of my money went to cocaine. I was living in my motor home in Lake Elsinore, a rural area east of Orange County. Because it was far from my job, Marilyn arranged for me to stay in her hotel at a decent rate, and I spent most of my time there. She continued to believe in me, and I was grateful for her big heart. But I wasn't sure my wild ways were a good long-term match for her squeaky-clean lifestyle.

Many of my drug connections were Latino guys from the heart of Los Angeles. One day, one of the guys I did business with approached me with a tempting proposition.

"Hey, I know a guy who's looking for a partner to go to Panama with him and smuggle some coke into the States," he told me.

"No, I don't want any part of that." I shook my head

adamantly. Movie clips of international drug smuggling — and long prison times — flashed through my mind.

But the guy introduced me to his friend Lyle, anyhow. "We have a different way of doing things," Lyle explained. "We convert the coke into liquid form and hide it in wine bottles. The drug-sniffing dogs can't smell it, and the customs officers working at the border aren't gonna bother to uncork the bottles. It's foolproof."

"Wow, that could work," I replied.

"We'll be gone only three days, and the job pays $5,000 on each end."

I gave a low whistle. "Wow, well, let me think about it, okay?" Christmas was just a couple weeks away. Did I want to risk getting stuck in Panama so close to the holidays? What if something went wrong? I went home that night and mulled it over. I could certainly use the money, and it did sound like a pretty foolproof idea. Where else was I going to come up with $10,000 that fast?

Lyle showed up at my door not long after with a substantial amount of drugs. "Consider it a down payment," he said. "Now are you in?"

I buckled under the pressure. He'd catered to my weakness. "Okay, let's do this thing," I agreed.

A few days later, I boarded a plane with my new partner, and we set off for Panama City. We got a hotel, and the next night, a Colombian man showed up at the door with two suitcases. Lyle spoke with him for a few minutes before the man handed the suitcases over. He then closed the door and turned to me.

"Well, Kurt, that wine bottle thing didn't work out after all," he said. "But we have these two suitcases here."

I stared at the small hard plastic suitcase. "So where's the drugs?"

"Inside the walls of the suitcase." Lyle popped it open and showed me the inside. It looked like nothing more than an empty piece of luggage.

"Wow, you're kidding." *This is not good, but what can I do? I hope it actually works.*

"You'll put your stuff in there," he explained. "And we'll head to the airport like a couple of tourists tomorrow morning and be on our way."

I shrugged as though I did this sort of stuff all the time. *What choice do I have?* "Here we go," I muttered.

Lyle purchased a number of items to put in my suitcase, intending to fool the x-ray technicians. One was an aerosol can.

The next day, Lyle and I headed to the airport to board the plane. We planned to land in Tijuana, Mexico, and split up. He would then smuggle the drugs through the Tijuana border, while I caught a ride with a friend. I checked my bags, my heart racing a bit as I thought of the mass amount of cocaine stuffed into the walls of the suitcase I held. *Just be cool,* I told myself. *Smile and blend in with the crowd.*

We boarded the plane, and I was surprised to discover Lyle had put me in first class while he sat in coach. Just before the plane left the gate, an airline employee approached me.

"Señor, we have a problem with your baggage," she said in Spanish. "I need you to come with me."

Gee, what problem could they possibly have with my bag? I attempted a straight face as I followed her back toward the gate. Inside, my heart thumped wildly in my chest. I'd thought if anything we'd have trouble at the U.S. border, not in Panama. *Just play it cool, Kurt. Act like nothing's wrong.*

"Señor, can you please open these suitcases?" the employee instructed.

To allay suspicion, I turned to the case with the drugs first. But I could not pry it open. *Lyle must have locked it, and I don't have the combination. Oops. No. No. Come on!* I tried again, but it would not budge. I could feel all eyes on me as I struggled to stay calm. I knew the scenario must look suspicious. *What am I gonna do now?*

"I think I have the combination written down back at my seat," I told the employees. "Can I go back and get it?"

They nodded, and I strode back to the plane and went directly to Lyle in his seat. "What's the combination?" I asked breathlessly.

But to my shock, Lyle glanced up and looked as though he'd never seen me before. Just then, a police officer entered the plane, and the next few moments became a blur of confusion. Lyle began speaking in Spanish, waving his hands and claiming, "I don't know this guy!" as he pointed to me.

"Both of you, come here," the cop barked.

My heart thudded so fast I feared it might jump out of

my chest. *This is not good.* As we followed the cop off the plane, a million scenarios played in my mind. This was supposed to be an easy gig — foolproof! Nothing was supposed to go wrong!

"Tell the cop we just met on a layover in Costa Rica," Lyle whispered to me as we shuffled back toward the gate. "Tell him you asked me to translate for you. Just trust me, okay?"

"Okay," I whispered back. But I didn't trust him at all. We were in serious trouble, and I knew it.

The cops marched in front and behind as we followed them down a flight of stairs toward the police headquarters. I felt like we were marching toward the death chamber. Utter fear gripped me, swallowing me up with each dreaded step. *This is as bad as it gets.*

We stepped inside the police headquarters, and Lyle and I stood next to each other. I tried not to make eye contact with the police officers as they hovered over us. With wide spike-brimmed hats, big guns with ammunition clips, a thick stripe down the side of their pants and a sash over their shoulders, they were an especially intimidating sight. They crossed their dark-skinned arms and glared at me from beneath greasy dark hair, and I tried to keep my cool. *Don't let them get to you, Kurt. Just keep calm.*

One of the cops took a large screwdriver and forced the lock of the first suitcase open. I gulped as he moved the contents around and started taking items out one by one. The large aerosol can rolled onto the table. Lyle had purposely packed items with specific shapes to cause a distraction while going through the x-ray machines. But apparently, it was the can that made the airline personnel want to see inside. After a few moments, I grew hopeful. *We might get away with this.*

And then, in one horrible motion, the cop punched the screwdriver through the side of the suitcase, and the white substance floated out. My heart sank. *I am in trouble.*

The cop put the substance into a test tube to confirm its contents. I watched with dread as he shook the tube, and it turned a certain color.

"Heroína," he announced.

"Heroin?" I hissed at Lyle, my angry eyes pleading an explanation.

"I don't know," Lyle whispered, shrugging innocently.

This presented a new set of problems. First, I knew the penalty for smuggling heroin was much more severe than smuggling cocaine. Second, I should have been paid twice as much for carrying heroin. And third, it was now clear that I had been had.

Would Lyle have really paid me and let me go in Tijuana? A thought struck me. *Maybe that aerosol can saved my life.*

"I don't know this guy," Lyle muttered as the cops led him away.

We were separated and interrogated privately by a plainclothes detective. "You want to explain this?" he asked, not mincing words.

"I bought the suitcases from a taxi driver at the hotel where I was staying," I stammered. "I had no idea what was in them."

The agent smiled and looked at me. "That's an amusing story, Señor. Would you like to tell me the truth?"

I sighed. "Okay, that was my suitcase, and I knew it had drugs."

The agent nodded. He brought the American consul representative into the room with a DEA agent to interview me, and I told them the truth. "Yes, I knew the suitcase was full of drugs," I confessed. "And I'm willing to work with you. But I need protection from that other guy, okay? I was working with him. I can't wind up in the same prison." At this point all bets were off. I needed to look out for myself.

The agents took us up to the headquarters and threw us into a large holding cell. Roughly 20 feet by 20 feet, it included concrete walls with bars and a toilet and shower in a corner. Six other people occupied the cell, and on the other side of the wall was another cell where women were locked up.

I spent the next week in the cell with Lyle, acting as if nothing was wrong between us. Everything had happened so quickly, I'd barely had time to process it. But now, as I sat against the hard concrete walls, the reality of my situation sank in. *I'm stuck in a cell in a foreign country for smuggling drugs. I've just missed Christmas with my family because I did something incredibly stupid. I have no idea what's going to happen next. This is not good at all.*

A lawyer sauntered in one day to speak with me. A slick fellow who went by the name of Mario, he spoke English well. "I want to help you," he said. "Let me contact your family and tell them you are here."

Figuring I didn't have many better options, I agreed to let him help me. He called my parents and told them where I was. They were relieved to know I was alive, as I hadn't shown up to celebrate Christmas. I knew I'd disappointed them greatly and that there would be many questions to answer when I got home. But for now, I'd have to wait to learn my fate.

After a week, the officials loaded me and another guy into the back of a Nissan Pathfinder and drove us out into the jungle. My co-passenger was an African-American guy named Javon from Tennessee. He seemed friendly enough, and I was grateful for the company. A warm rain dusted the dirt roads as we entered the lush green rainforest. Under any other circumstances, this would have been one of the most beautiful places I had ever seen. The driver swerved all over the road, and we braced ourselves the best we could, handcuffs and all. *This ride seems like punishment enough,* I thought wryly. *We'll be lucky to show up alive wherever we're going.*

We arrived at a large compound surrounded by a barbed-wire fence. An old building with a rusty steel roof and no windows sat amidst the beautiful tropical paradise. The guards let me and Javon out of the vehicle and handcuffed us to the railing of the building. *This must be some sort of prison facility.*

I glanced around, noticing several other large buildings surrounded by a chain-link fence. One looked like an old stucco Latin American church. Rows of structures with palm-grass roofs sat beside two large warehouse-type structures. The entire area seemed to encompass 3 or 4 acres. As we stood there handcuffed to the building, a light, warm rain pelted our faces. To my amazement, as I gazed beyond the buildings, I saw a huge ship coming toward us. It appeared to be cruising between the hills on land. *What on earth?* And then I realized we must be right next to the Panama Canal. From a distance, the waterway was invisible. I had never seen anything like it in my life. This scene would repeat itself many times. Cruise ships regularly traversed the canal, close enough that I could wave at the passengers, imagining the endless buffets of food they enjoyed. They took my picture. They knew why I was there. I felt ashamed.

I am really in deep trouble. I've screwed up really badly. The reality of my dire situation suddenly hit me with force. *I'm not getting to get out of this place anytime soon.*

The prison officials came to process us. As they led us down toward the security area, I felt all eyes on us. I continued down the path, my head held high. First impressions count. Showing weakness was a bad idea. *We are fresh meat. These prisoners are surely checking us out.* I knew Javon and I must look like quite a pair — me, a clean-cut white guy and he, a well-dressed black man. We followed the officials into the older of the two large structures. The size of a small grocery store, it resembled a large warehouse. Several cage-type structures lined the walls. They ushered us to the far corner of the building, and immediately, a pungent smell hit my nostrils. I winced.

The officials threw us into a dark, rusty, dirty cell, which appeared to be the worst accommodations in the place. Steel bunks that looked as though they'd been salvaged from an old ship served as the only furniture inside our new accommodations. I'd never felt so empty or alone. We'd come with very little. For me, that included a bag with a pair of pants and a shirt, as well as the jeans and t-shirt on my back. The laces had been removed from my shoes. I had no pillow or blanket, and the steel bunks were completely bare.

This is it. My new home. I gulped hard, taking in the cold, barren surroundings. I'd lived in many places over the years, but I'd never seen anything like this. Even my motor home back in Lake Elsinore seemed like the Hyatt compared to these sparse conditions. *This is what you get for screwing up, Kurt. You've done it now.*

This area of the prison system was called Reflección. The guards held new prisoners in these cells incommunicado for three weeks, while the authorities evaluated how well they got along with the prison population. During that time, they also investigated the pending charges. If we exhibited good behavior, we'd have a chance to eventually move out and experience a bit more freedom. But for now, we were isolated.

Soon a Puerto Rican-American kid stopped by, his dark brown eyes meeting mine. "What do you need?"

"Well, I left all my drugs at the airport," I replied dryly.

"Here." He handed me some toilet paper. "You'll need this. It ain't so bad in here."

I hadn't even thought about simple necessities like toilet paper. I accepted it gratefully, then glanced at the hole in the ground in the corner of the cell. *This is the toilet? There's no privacy? Well, I guess I'm going to have to forgo all inhibitions in here.*

As I walked barefoot to the showers one day, a stranger in another cell handed me a pair of sandals. "You never wanna walk to the showers barefoot," he informed me. "You could get some nasty infection." My heart warmed at his generosity.

These guys aren't exactly my friends, but they're all I have right now, so I might as well be cool and make the best of things while I'm in here, I decided.

While I avoided many of the tougher-looking guys, I also formed some surprising friendships during my incarceration.

One day, a bald-headed black guy from Barbados showed up in my cell. With thick dark rings under his eyes and a hardened look on his face, he refused to smile as he introduced himself. After telling us he'd come from a nasty prison in another city, he said little else.

This guy is a force to be reckoned with, I decided,

surveying his look from head to toe. But something in me decided to try to crack him open. During my time inside the prison, I'd learned that many of these guys were really not so different than me after all. Many had come from decent homes and had never expected to find themselves in a grimy prison cell. I approached him and initiated a conversation.

"It's tough in here," I told him. "You know, I haven't even spoken to my mom yet." I worried that she might never speak to me again.

The guy glanced up at me and stared me down with his dark, unruly eyes. "You listen to me," he said in a thick accent. "This is the woman who bore the pain of childbirth for you. You call your mother, you tell her you love her. And that you're sorry."

I was taken aback by his words. "Okay, I will," I promised.

Javon found a deck of cards and created a game with cardboard called "Race." Each day, he called out, asking who wanted to play. He turned that little deck of cards into an entrepreneurial endeavor and began raking in the cash. I soon learned that he was not the only one scheming to make money inside the prison. Currency was allowed inside, and everyone seemed to be out to make a few bucks.

At night, I huddled on the grimy steel bunk, trying to fall asleep. Everything, from the rusty bars to the dirty floor, was disgusting. I cringed as several huge cockroaches flitted under my feet. My mind wandered to

Marilyn back home. I would have killed for a warm bed and a clean floor in her hotel about now.

All for a suitcase full of drugs, Kurt. How stupid could you have been?

Breakfast included a stale biscuit, a hard-boiled egg and a cup of lukewarm tea. Lunch was a bland combination of rice and beans or a hotdog. Once a week, the cooks offered chicken. I soon learned the guys in the prison went crazy for chicken. They did anything they could to get their hands on a piece of the meat. I decided it wasn't worth fighting over. I'd stick to my hotdog and beans.

I lost track of time as the days stretched into weeks. I remained civil with my cellmates, though most of them made it clear they weren't happy to have a husky 6-foot-tall American guy around. After the United States invaded Panama 10 years prior, anti-American sentiment ran high. I soon learned that standing up to a "gringo" was considered a badge of honor. As they stared me down and initiated trouble, I tried my best to avoid them.

It was never more evident than the day I accidentally spilled tea on my new cellmate, a former boxing trainer. Paulo beat me to a pulp for my trouble, but not without the other prisoners noticing that I was able to defend myself. While I definitely lost the fight, the incident earned me some "prison cred" and gave me a measure of peace and protection, since most inmates left me alone after that. It wasn't worth a brawl if the gringo fought back.

A month after being admitted, I received my first court date. I pled guilty. Lyle, however, pled not guilty. Many months later, I received a second court date. I stood before a judge in a muggy little office space as he sat at his desk. There was no jury. I learned that my case would be decided by how well he got along with my lawyer. In Panama, the judge had the ultimate say, no questions asked.

A pastor pulled up to the prison one day in an old 1970 Dodge Colt. He gave an English-speaking Bible study, and I eagerly went to the meeting.

"Let me guess why you are here," he said as we chatted briefly before the meeting.

"Well, they didn't like my choice of souvenirs at the airport," I replied, cracking a wry smile.

Pastor Wilbur visited often, leading us in a time of worship and reading out of the Bible. His words and music encouraged me greatly. Being stuck in a filthy prison in a foreign country with a bunch of guys who didn't like Americans was often lonely and scary. For the first time since arriving, I felt a glimmer of hope. To my surprise, many other guys from the prison showed up, too, wanting to hear about God's love. I looked forward to the pastor's visits every week. He brought tasty sandwiches and cloves of garlic, two treats we savored. He also facilitated mail and other forms of communication between prisoners and their families back home.

"Keep studying your Bible," he told me. "There's a wealth of helpful information in there."

TOTAL RESTORATION

One day, the pastor brought me a guitar. The instrument was obviously cheap, but I was overjoyed all the same. I had desperately missed playing the guitar, and at last I'd have something to keep me busy when the muggy days grew long.

I soon learned the game of bribery behind bars. We could hang out on the patio outside by simply slipping the hallway cop a dollar. The guy made a decent living collecting money from guys who needed a little fresh air. I dutifully paid him my dollars and spent my afternoons on the covered patio, taking in some much-needed sunshine and playing my new guitar. It was a small step toward freedom and a welcome escape from the dreary, cramped quarters inside.

Drugs flowed just as freely inside the prison as they did outside. Many guys managed to smuggle cocaine, marijuana and other substances into their cells. I stayed away from the drugs, as they were the very reason I'd landed here in the first place. I knew if I stayed on my best behavior I'd stand a much better chance of getting out sooner.

As the days dragged by, I learned the ropes of the system. I was not fond of my cellmates and determined to find some new guys to bunk with.

I met a couple European guys, and we paid off the right people to get our own cell. I now bunked with two Germans, two Spaniards and two Americans.

One of the Spaniards was the music director in the Catholic church on the prison grounds. He taught me many of the Spanish Catholic songs. Soon he was released, and I became the Director of Music for the prison's Catholic church, the building I spotted when I first arrived.

This was a turning point. Now I had friends, protection and privileges as part of the church everyone respected. I was able to stay on the patio all day every day. Those I selected for my church choir got the same privileges.

One day, a guy named Luis approached me. A large, intimidating black guy from Panama, Luis had been a notorious gang leader on the streets of Panama. He bossed the guards around, and they didn't mess with him.

"Hey, Kurt, one of my homeboys wants to be in your choir," Luis barked at me. "Sings real good, you know what I'm saying?"

"He's in," I replied, wanting to appease him. Luis was known for conducting lots of business inside the prison. If anyone needed a favor, he knew to take care of Luis first. I wanted to make every effort to stay on his good side — no matter how badly his friend sang.

When I wasn't busy playing guitar on the patio, I spent time watching TV inside. Only two stations came in at the prison, so our viewing choices were limited. We used rabbit ears and ran wire to get better reception. But one guy was especially brilliant. He brought in a nice antenna, much like the ones I'd seen on roofs years before. He set up a cable system and offered subscriptions for $5 a week. His business boomed as guys lined up to hand over their cash in exchange for extended viewing pleasures. Later he obtained a VCR for pay-per-view shows.

The two highlights of my prison time were the patio and Bible study. While sitting on a hard bucket on the patio, it occurred to me that there had to be a way to make these things more comfortable. I'd learned a thing or two about upholstery in the upholstery shop on the prison grounds and figured I could come up with something handy. I began creating cushions for the buckets using old foam I found on the beds after prisoners got released. I fashioned them into a decent, comfortable seat, and the other guys were impressed. The project gave me something to do and also secured a niche for me in the underground entrepreneurial world at the prison.

There was a pay phone on the patio, which guys often used to make collect calls. I called my mother, and she expressed her relief over the line.

"I am so glad to hear from you, Kurt. I've been so worried about you," she cried. "Listen. I'm praying for you every single day. Don't go so long without calling me, okay? Call once a week, if you can."

"It's nice to hear your voice, Mom," I said wistfully. I pictured my mother's face, etched with concern as she gripped the phone thousands of miles away. I longed to see my family again. I'd do everything I could to get released as soon as possible.

I went back to court again to be sentenced. I received a sentence of 72 months. The length was a hard blow. Afterward, they loaded me into an old minivan with three

Panamanian guards, and we bumped along the road back to the prison. I spotted a McDonald's up ahead and began salivating. Hard-boiled eggs and hotdogs were starting to get old. "Can we pull in there, guys? I'll buy," I requested.

We pulled into the drive-thru, and I bought all the guards Big Mac combos. As I bit into my hamburger, I savored every bite, grateful for a little taste of home away from home. We pulled over on the side of the road and got rid of the evidence before returning to the prison. I made three good friends that night, and the incident made me chuckle whenever I thought about it.

I continued to go to Bible study, play my guitar and pray. I learned the translation for the prison's name, Cárcel Renacer. "Nacer" means "to be born," and "renacer" means "to be born again." This struck me as especially significant. While I considered myself a praying man, I'd never truly leaned on God with all my heart. I'd spent much of my life making selfish in-the-moment choices, not thinking much about the consequences. I'd used God like a lifeboat, going to him only when I was in trouble. But now, for the first time, I understood what it fully meant to have a meaningful relationship with God. In the midst of grimy bunk beds, fistfights, cockroaches, nasty food and long, lonely nights, I'd discovered true hope and peace. My conditions were far from ideal, but I knew I was not alone. I also knew that life didn't end on this earth. Because I'd invited God into my heart, I could spend eternity with him in heaven, where there was no sorrow or suffering. Knowing this life was not all I had helped me make the most out of my mundane days in prison. While I wanted to be set free, I also knew I needed this time to refocus, get my priorities straight and grow close to God. Prison was better than any rehab program I could have checked myself into back home. Drugs were not the answer — Jesus was. And if I kept my eyes on him, I'd truly be set free.

One day, the pastor, who'd been communicating with my family, gave me some bad news. "Your brother has advanced prostate cancer. He is not doing well," he told me.

My brother, Pat, had left Southern California years before to open up a business in Cottage Grove, Oregon, followed there by my parents. He had a loving wife and three sons. The idea of never seeing him again was devastating.

"God, I really want to see my brother before he dies," I prayed. "Please make a way for that to happen."

God soon answered my prayers. I left the Panamanian prison in 2003, nearly three years after I first entered, bound for the Detention Center in Miami. I was led, handcuffed, by armed guards out of that place to be repatriated, and I glanced back one last time. I thought of Javon, Luis, my friend from Barbados, and everyone else I'd met behind bars. I thought of Pastor Wilbur and how we'd teased him about his beat-up old car as it rattled down the road. I thought of my friends in the choir, of the many times we'd sat outside on the patio while I strummed my cheap little guitar and sang. There had been several harrowing moments, for sure. But I'd also discovered a sense of camaraderie among my fellow inmates. We each arrived bearing our own scars; we each had a story to share. But in the end, I discovered we weren't so different after all. We were all just a bunch of broken guys in need of a Savior. I'd found my Savior, Jesus Christ, and I prayed many of them would, too. I'd most likely never see them again on this earth, but perhaps I'd see a few of them in heaven someday.

The U.S. Marshal flew me from Panama to Miami, Florida. I joined several other men and women also bound for the United States. When we landed, several vans with blackened windows arrived to pick us up. *This is the first time I've ridden in a decent vehicle since my arrest,* I mused as I climbed into the van.

We headed to the Miami Detention Center, a nondescript building not far away, overlooking Biscayne Bay — with a million-dollar view. There, I joined several other non-violent people who had been locked up for a variety of crimes, including money laundering and theft. Some 100 guys shared one unit, and there were two levels of rooms with no bars. The facility offered recreational activities, like handball and music, and a bank of six TVs ran across the ceiling. I learned I'd stay there until I was resentenced according to the U.S. guidelines. The difference from prison in Panama was incredible. I thought I'd landed in Disney World.

Grateful to be back on U.S. soil, I obeyed all the rules at the detention center and waited for further instructions.

TOTAL RESTORATION

At last, I received a phone call from the corrections office. I got a Greyhound bus ticket from Miami to Cottage Grove, and the center released me. I boarded the bus wearing a sweat suit and tennis shoes I'd purchased at the commissary. I had no other possessions. Once I arrived in Oregon, I'd have to completely start my life over.

I was impressed with the pretty little town of Cottage Grove. Not far from Eugene, it boasted lush greenery, rambling blackberry bushes, stunning sunsets and gorgeous mountain views. I reunited with my brother, and we spent days catching up. I shared my prison stories with him, and he shared his health struggles with me. He was growing weak, and the doctors were not optimistic about finding a cure for his cancer. I was grateful God had given me the chance to spend his last days with him.

I went to work at my brother's shop, and one of my friends introduced me to Calvary Chapel Eugene nearby. After a few visits, the church invited me to come join the worship team. I was excited to use the talents God had given me, playing guitar and singing. Though the environment was very different than the prison patio, the idea was the same. I now believed that no matter where I went God could use me.

In 2004, my brother sold his shop shortly before he passed away. I grieved him terribly, as did the rest of my family. My mother, always cheerful and optimistic, could hardly get herself out of bed for months. It struck me as ironic that while I'd been the troublesome brother, Pat had always been the straight shooter — a real family man.

It saddened me to watch his widow and children grieve. I wished we'd had more time together, but I was still thankful for the memories.

I attended the local community college and received my GED. I got a job at a glass shop and bought my first home in 2009. Situated on a small piece of land, the place included several fruit trees and brilliant sunflowers. I soon gained the reputation for having the best lawn in the neighborhood. *Thank you, God. I never dreamed I'd be a homeowner someday. Your goodness is beyond what I could ever ask for or imagine.* I would never take any of my blessings for granted again. I knew I did not deserve this new life. I'd done some terribly selfish things over the years. But God offered a clean slate. He did not remind me of my past mistakes or berate me when I screwed up. Instead, he lovingly, patiently helped me stay on the right path. I was not an ex-prisoner in his eyes — I was his forgiven son. And knowing that was the best feeling in the world.

৯৯৯৯

"Come on, Dad, you ready?" I called out.

"Yep, comin'." My dad, now 83 years old, grabbed his golf clubs and followed me to the car.

It was a brilliant Oregon day, and I'd decided to go golfing with my dad. My parents owned a house just a few streets over from mine, and I helped my mother landscape her yard in my spare time. After being separated from them for so long, I now treasured every single day together.

I was now involved in three different churches playing worship. I'd begun attending Living Faith Assembly of God after discovering it down the street from my house one day. I loved playing at the Saturday night service and enjoyed the pastor's casual approach. He made every single person who walked through the door feel welcome. I thanked God for my new friends who loved God and loved me. Many of them were shocked to learn I'd spent time in prison. Clean-cut, with no tattoos, I knew I didn't look like the typical ex-con. But my story helped me remember to never judge people at first glance. While their life may look perfect on the outside, they may have their own set of battle wounds.

I'd gotten back in touch with Marilyn after moving back, and she'd invited me down for the Fourth of July. Still a successful businesswoman, she was happy to see me. We reminisced and had fun catching up, and I thanked God for bringing that relationship full circle. Marilyn had played an instrumental part in bringing me to God by inviting me to church, and I will be forever grateful for her.

As my dad and I neared the golf course, I thanked God once again for bringing me to Oregon. Here, I'd found meaningful relationships, churches that I loved, astounding beauty, a great job and a true sense of peace. I would never forget my time behind bars, as it had changed me forever. Ironically, it was behind those bars that God set me free, long before I was released. There, I'd found a lasting hope, and I would carry that with me for the rest of my life.

CONCLUSION

When I became a pastor, my desire was to see lives transformed. My hope was to see people encouraged and the hurting filled with hope. As I read this book, I saw that passion being fulfilled. However, at Living Faith, rather than being content with our past victories, we are spurred to believe that many more can occur.

Every time we see another changed life, it increases our awareness that God really loves people, and he is actively seeking to change lives. Think about it: How did you get this book? We believe you read this book because God brought it to you seeking to reveal his love to you. Whether you're a man or a woman, a logger or a waitress, a mechanic or a school bus driver, a parent or a student, we believe God came to save you. He came to save us. He came to save them. He came to save all of us from the hellish pain we've wallowed in. He came to offer real change and a new kind of life that will last forever through faith in Jesus Christ.

Do you have honest questions that such radical change is possible? It seems too good to be true, doesn't it? Each of us at Living Faith warmly invites you to come and check out our church family. Freely ask questions, examine our beliefs and see if we're "for real." And if you choose, journey with us at whatever pace you are comfortable. You will find that we are far from perfect.

TOTAL RESTORATION

Our scars and sometimes open wounds are still healing, but we just want you to know that we are actively involved in this process of restoration. We still make mistakes in our journey, like everyone will. Therefore, we acknowledge our continued need for each other's forgiveness and support. We need the love of God just as much as we did the day before we believed in him.

If you are unable to be part of our family, yet you intuitively sense you would really like to experience such a life change, here are some basic thoughts to consider. If you choose, when you are done reading, you can pray the suggested prayer. If your prayer genuinely comes from the heart, you will experience the beginning stages of authentic life change, similar to those you have read about.

How does this change occur?

Recognize that what you're doing isn't working. Accept the fact that Jesus desires to forgive you for your bad decisions and selfish motives. Realize that without this forgiveness, you will continue a life separated from God and his amazing love. In the Bible, the book of Romans, chapter 6, verse 23 reads, "The result of sin (seeking our way rather than God's way) is death, but the gift that God freely gives is everlasting life found in Jesus Christ."

Believe in your heart that God passionately loves you and wants to give you a new heart. Ezekiel 11:19 reads, "I will give them singleness of heart and put a new spirit within them. I will take away their stony, stubborn heart and give them a tender, responsive heart" (NLT).

CONCLUSION

Believe in your heart that "if you confess with your mouth that Jesus is Lord and believe in your heart that God raised him from the dead, you will be saved" (Romans 10:9 NLT).

Believe in your heart that because Jesus paid for your failure and wrong motives, and because you asked him to forgive you, he has filled your new heart with his life in such a way that he transforms you from the inside out. Second Corinthians 5:17 reads, "When someone becomes a Christian, he becomes a brand new person inside. He is not the same anymore. A new life has begun!"

Why not pray something like this right now?

Lord Jesus, if I've learned one thing in my journey, it's that you are God and I am not. My choices have not resulted in the happiness I hoped they would bring. Not only have I experienced pain, I've also caused it. I know I am separated from you, but I want that to change. I am sorry for the choices I've made that have hurt myself and those I love. I believe your death paid for my sins, and you are now alive to change me from the inside out. Would you please do that now? I want to experience this total restoration. I ask you to come and live in me so that I can sense you are here with me. Thank you for hearing and changing me. Now please help me know when you are talking to me, so I can cooperate with your efforts to change me. Amen.

TOTAL RESTORATION

Living Faith's unfolding story of God's love is still being written. Now that you have read their stories, we would love for you to come and *meet* the people who lived them.

We hope to see you this weekend!

Rulon Combs — Lead Pastor
Living Faith Assembly of God
Cottage Grove, Oregon

We would love for you to join us at Living Faith Assembly of God!

We meet Sunday mornings at 10:30 a.m. at 467 S. 10th Street, Cottage Grove, OR 97424.

E Main St

S 10th St

S Pacific Hwy

I-5

Join us for our Saturday night service called "The Bridge," which is at 6 p.m.

Please call us at 541.942.2612 for directions, or contact us at www.livingfaithag.com.

For more information on reaching your city with
stories from your church, go to
www.testimonybooks.com.

Good Catch
Publishing

Did one of these stories touch you?
Did one of these real people move you to tears?
Tell us (and them) about it on our Facebook page at
www.facebook.com/GoodCatchPublishing.